What Everyone Knew.

What Everyone Knew.

Inside the Failures Organizations See
Coming and Don't Stop.

Cristian Y. Gonzalez

C.Y. Gonzalez

Published by:
C.Y. Gonzalez
Houston, Texas

ISBN 979-8-9958067-0-7 (hardcover)
ISBN 979-8-9958067-1-4 (paperback)
ISBN 979-8-9958067-2-1 (ebook)

Printed in the United States of America

To my wife, for her steady support, and to my sons, who will one day see their own versions of this.

What Everyone Knew.

Inside the Failures Organizations See Coming and Don't Stop.

Contents

Introduction

Over the course of my career, I have watched hundreds of millions of dollars in value disappear, not because organizations lacked talent, resources, or technical capability, but because of behaviors we all recognize and still allow to happen.

Corporate politics, toxic positivity, the illusion of progress — patterns most of us have seen and often participated in. The collapse of honest dialogue under the weight of self-preservation. These are not exotic failures; they are ordinary ones. They happen in companies of every size, in industries of every kind, and they repeat themselves with a consistency that should disturb anyone paying attention.

What still surprises me is not the failures, but how much we manage to accomplish despite how reliably we sabotage ourselves. And what drives me is the question underneath that observation: how much further could we go if we stopped behaving in such a way?

This book is an attempt to name those behaviors clearly and stop them before they become expensive.

If you have led work where different groups had to stay aligned through months or years of execution, you have seen this. Not once. Many times. This book is for those still in it.

The patterns I'm describing are not industry-specific. I have watched them play out in startups, in corporate transformations, in joint ventures, in non-profits. But I am going to show them to you primarily through one environment: complex, high-stakes industrial projects. Not because the lessons live there, but because that is where leadership failures that would otherwise stay subtle become dramatic and expensive. Where the gap between what leaders believe about their organizations and what is actually happening inside them gets exposed, sometimes catastrophically. Where the bill for poor leadership always comes due.

They rarely appear where people expect them.

Sometimes the first sign that something is wrong inside an organization doesn't show up in the work at all. It shows up earlier — sometimes before the work has even begun.

A former colleague texted me one morning on WhatsApp, asking when I might have time for a call. I was expecting it. A mutual friend had mentioned he might reach out. We had worked together on several projects over the years. I knew how he operated. He knew how I operated. There was trust.

On the call he described what he was dealing with. I had done that exact kind of work before, and I told him so. It sounded like a straightforward engagement, good for his company and good for mine. A win-win, the way it was being described. I put together a proposal. He said the number worked and that he wanted to move forward.

Another former colleague of ours had recently joined the same company to handle contracts. I knew him too. I trusted him. It felt like the kind of situation that was meant to work out. He reviewed the proposal, said it was fair, and routed it to legal.

That was when the story started diverging from the one I thought I was in.

Legal came back and said the company used its own master service agreement and I would need to work from their document. That was not unusual. What was unusual was the document itself. It was written for people who do trade work at industrial facilities — the kind of work where you show up in steel-toed boots and turn valves with wrenches. That wasn't what we were going to do. Every protection went to the company, every exposure to the contractor. It wasn't a slanted starting point. It was aggressive enough that I kept thinking the same thing as I read: who in their right mind would sign this?

I redlined it and sent it back. The response should have been straightforward — we had already agreed on the key terms in our earlier conversations, before legal had ever entered the picture. What came back instead was strange, not just adjusted but walking back positions we had already settled. I was still processing that when a second revision landed in my inbox. Two revisions of the same document. Different directions. Different lawyers. Same contract.

I called my contact. He didn't have an answer. He said he needed to go figure out what was happening on their side.

That was the moment my understanding shifted. Up to that point, it had felt like a messy negotiation. After that, it felt like no one over there was really in control.

And I kept going.

The next few months were more of the same. Redlines going back and forth. Positions relitigated. Response times lengthening.

That is the part I think about most now. Not the dysfunction on their side, but the fact that I kept going. I extended myself further than I would have for any other client because this wasn't any other client. A friend had called me. Another friend was trying to push it through on the inside. I wanted it to work, and I wanted it to work for them as much as for me. So when the signals started piling up, I didn't stop and ask the question I would have asked for a stranger: what is this actually telling me?

My WhatsApp messages to my friend started changing around that point, not hostile, just shorter. Instead of checking in, I was asking whether this was going to happen at all. The replies got slower, then inconsistent.

At the six-month mark, I sent him a message that was close to blunt. I was done with the pleasantries. I told him I needed to know where things stood. He said he was busy. He would call me within a week.

He did.

I don't remember the exact words. I remember the shape of the call. He didn't start with an apology. He started by explaining, slowly, what had actually been happening inside his company. Assets acquired at costs that could never be recovered. Decisions made in sequence, each one defensible in isolation, none of them adding up to a business that worked. Capital committed so far past the point of no return that the math alone made the situation unworkable.

They had facilities. They had production. What they didn't have was a path to profitability.

Every contract was on hold. Every hire was on hold. There had been no contract to award, not to me, not to anyone, for months. The process I had been pushing through wasn't slow. It was irrelevant.

He didn't make excuses. He came clean. I still respect him for it.

And then, sitting with it after we hung up, I had the thought that has stayed with me longer than anything else about that engagement.

The problems he had just described to me — the decisions made without alignment, the information that never surfaced in time, the reality the organization couldn't allow itself to see — were not the problems he had called me to solve. He had called me for something narrower. But the deeper failure, the one that had put the company where it was, was exactly the kind of work we do. If we had been brought in two years earlier, before the bad decisions hardened into commitments, there was a real chance none of this would have happened.

I told him that on the call. It wasn't the moment for it, but I told him anyway.

He knew.

I've seen that pattern repeat across organizations and industries. The details change. The structure doesn't. And it almost never starts as a technical problem.

The real problem in that story had happened long before the contract arrived. It was in how decisions had been made, how information had moved, and how reality had been allowed to surface inside the organization. Or more accurately, how it hadn't. By the time the dysfunction became visible from the outside, the outcome had already been set. The contract was just where it showed up.

That is what this book is about.

There is no ill intent assumed anywhere in these pages. The failures described here are not the result of bad people; I've been part of some of them myself, sometimes seeing it clearly, sometimes only understanding it later. They are the result of fear, ego, misaligned incentives, and the entirely human tendency to protect what we have rather than build what we could.

The cost of that tendency is measured in millions. In capital that doesn't earn its return, throughput that doesn't materialize, and schedules that absorb the difference between what was promised and what gets delivered.

It doesn't have to be.

This book is built around a simple observation: *the same leadership failures repeat themselves across organizations with remarkable consistency.* They follow a recognizable sequence, what I have come to call *"the failure sequence"*.

First, clarity breaks down. The organization loses a shared understanding of what it is trying to accomplish, or never establishes one. Decisions that should be simple become difficult. Teams hesitate on what to do next. The explanations you hear for the hesitation don't quite line up with what you understand about the work.

That loss creates misalignment. Different groups begin optimizing for different objectives without anyone noticing. Deliverables come back off-target. Functions produce numbers that take real work to reconcile. Objectives between groups turn out to be incompatible.

Then truth stops flowing. Culture shifts from candor to self-preservation. The environment leaders have built, intentionally or not, begins filtering the information they receive. You start noticing the signs at the edges of meetings — the awkward silence after a question, the glance exchanged across the table, the unevenly raised eyebrow, the careful answer that arrives a beat slower than it should. Problems become invisible until they become expensive.

Then specific forces erode what remains. Governance weakens. Processes become performative. Infighting and political argument replace decisions. Direction starts coming from people who weren't in the original structure. Each of these can happen independently, but they tend to compound.

In the ideal world, this is prevented from happening in the first place. But in the real world, often someone has to lead through the damage.

That is the failure sequence.

The Failure Sequence

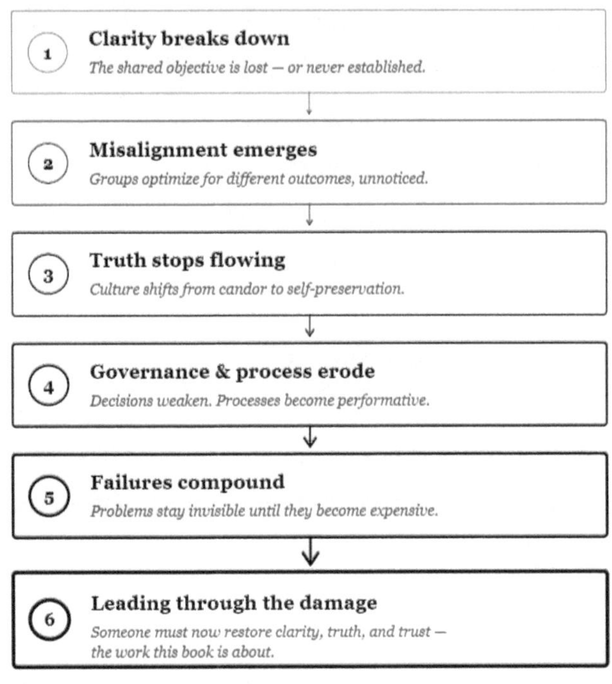

Each stage is harder, slower, and more costly to reverse than the one before it.

The failure sequence shows up often enough that it's worth understanding, and it is the structure of this book.

Part I examines how clarity is established, maintained, and lost — and how that loss creates misalignment that pulls even capable teams apart.

Part II examines the environment that determines whether truth reaches the people who need it, and what happens when it doesn't.

Part III examines the specific forces — governance, process, and culture — that erode both clarity and truth, and how they compound when left unaddressed.

Part IV asks what leadership actually looks like when someone has to work through the damage, and what it costs when no one does.

My hope is that this book does several things at once.

For those responsible for the outcome — the leaders who will live with the consequences of the decisions being made around them — it offers a way to see more clearly. To recognize when the organization is operating the way you believe it is, and when it isn't.

For those who can see the problem clearly but cannot safely say so: it gives you a reference point. Something you can point to or share, that makes the issue visible without forcing you to carry it alone.

And for those who sense that something is wrong but cannot name it: it gives you the language. Not theory. Specific, recognizable patterns drawn from real efforts, described clearly enough that you can identify them in your own organization.

If you lead anything — a company, a project, a team, a mission — these patterns are already operating around you. What follows is how to recognize them, and what it takes to lead through them.

Part I — The Foundation: Clarity

Everything that follows starts with a single loss: the organization no longer shares an understanding of what it is trying to accomplish.

Chapter 1

What Are We Trying to Accomplish?

You have sat in a meeting where everyone was working hard and nothing was getting done. That feeling is what this chapter is about.

Clarity is the ever-elusive, often ignored starting point.

Think of it like a car windshield. Keeping it clean is not a one-time task; it requires constant attention. The longer you drive without cleaning it, the more dirt accumulates, and the harder it becomes to see what's ahead.

Clarity in any organization works the same way. Counterintuitively, it is often obscured by the very activity meant to drive progress. Each new meeting, each new data point, each new stakeholder opinion adds another layer to the glass. Left unattended, what began as a clear shared objective becomes murky, and once it becomes murky, teams begin drifting. Each group rowing hard in the direction that makes the most sense from their own position, unaware that the others are rowing somewhere slightly different.

The result is wasted resources at best. At worst, it is an organization that has traveled a long distance in the wrong direction, too committed to its momentum to easily change course.

Every organization brings together people with different disciplines, different instincts, and different ways of seeing the same problem. When the objective is clear, those different viewpoints sharpen a decision. When it isn't, they pull against each other. Each one optimizing for its own version of success, each one entirely reasonable, and none of them producing the outcome the organization actually needs.

Clarity is the prerequisite for alignment. And without both, even the most capable teams can find themselves solving different versions of the same problem.

Recognizing Misalignment

I have been in that room many times. One in particular stays with me.

The meeting had been going on for nearly an hour. Around the table were some of the most experienced technical people in the facility: process engineers, operations leaders, plant management, and technical specialists. Drawings were on the screen, spreadsheets were circulating, and the conversation was energetic.

It was a front-end engineering meeting during the conceptual phase of a plant expansion in Colombia. I had been brought in to help lead a portion of the engineering effort because the project had stalled. Progress had slowed, decisions were not sticking, and the team was struggling to move forward.

Everyone in the room worked for the plant. These were not outside consultants or contractors. They were the people responsible for operating the facility and helping to deliver the expansion.

From the outside, the meeting looked exactly like what progress is supposed to look like. People were engaged. Ideas were being debated. Technical options were being analyzed.

But something about the discussion didn't feel right.

The conversation kept moving from one technical detail to another without ever settling on a clear direction. One moment the group was discussing the capacity of a piece of equipment. A few minutes later the focus shifted to operating flexibility. Then someone raised concerns about schedule risk.

Each point was valid on its own. Yet, taken together, the discussion felt strangely unfocused. Every time the group seemed close to a decision, the conversation would drift again.

Eventually the room reached a kind of gridlock.

At that point I stopped the conversation and looked around the table.

"Gentlemen," I said, "it would be a very difficult conversation for me to go back to headquarters and explain how the smartest people in this facility couldn't come up with a solution."

The room went quiet.

After a moment I asked a simple question.

"What exactly are we trying to accomplish?"

This time the room stayed quiet for a different reason.

One person answered first. Their explanation focused on the technology being developed. Another described the project in terms of reducing manufacturing cost. Someone else emphasized the strategic importance of the project to the company's future.

None of the answers were wrong.

But they weren't the same answer.

The project had talent. It had funding. It had technical expertise. What it didn't have was alignment.

What happened in that room is not unusual. I have seen the same room in many different contexts and industries. The technology was different. The dynamic was identical.

Misalignment rarely announces itself as open disagreement. It settles in beneath the surface, in the space between what each group is optimizing for.

Without a clearly defined and reinforced objective, each discipline begins optimizing according to the priorities that make sense within its own world, and each of those priorities is legitimate. The problem isn't that people are pursuing the wrong things. It's that they're pursuing different versions of the right thing, without anyone holding the shared direction that would calibrate all of them toward the same outcome.

One of the most revealing tools a leader can use is also one of the simplest: ask people what the effort is trying to accomplish. Not in a large meeting where everyone hears the same explanation, but individually. Ask across functions. Ask across levels. Ask the people executing the work and the people sponsoring it.

Then listen carefully to the answers.

When a team is truly aligned, the answers tend to converge. The wording may vary depending on each person's role, but the core idea remains consistent.

When alignment is missing, the answers begin to diverge. Imagine asking members of the same team what success looks like and hearing: "We need to do this at the lowest possible cost." And: "We need to move as quickly as possible, regardless of cost." And: "We need to design for maximum future flexibility." Each of those goals leads to different decisions. Pursued simultaneously without being reconciled, they pull the effort apart.

Sometimes the problem isn't said out loud. It emerges from the work, often later than anyone would have wanted.

On one joint venture between two companies, the commercial structure — ownership, operating responsibilities, cost allocation — was still being negotiated.

And yet the engineering effort was fully underway. Scope had been defined. Work had been assigned. From the outside, it looked like we were making progress.

From the inside, it felt like something was off.

Part of the problem was structural. Communication between the two organizations did not happen directly. There were designated points of contact on each side, and all interaction was expected to flow through them. By the time information came back, it had often lost context or urgency. Sometimes the replies didn't quite line up with what we had asked. We would send a specific technical question and get back something adjacent, close enough that you couldn't call it wrong, but not quite answering what we needed to know. At some point the gaps became impossible to ignore.

I asked for the commercial agreements — whatever was available — because we needed them to understand what we were actually designing against, what constraints and requirements we were working with. In previous projects, this had been standard practice. Sometimes the documents came with sensitive terms redacted, sometimes fully readable, but they always came. Here they didn't.

People came into meetings, issued instructions on the fly, and moved on. Different people gave conflicting instructions. Instructions were reversed the same way they were given — on the fly, by whoever walked in next. Nothing was written down. Nothing was traceable to a document anyone could point to. Things weren't adding up, and the more I pushed, the more I was sure they weren't going to — not without the contracts in front of us. I kept asking for them because I needed them to do my job, and most importantly because having them would have made it impossible to keep running the effort on assertions without backup. I was told in person I would get them. Every time I followed up, the story changed. What I kept getting were reassurances instead of documents, and even those kept shifting. The real and legal constraints we were supposed to be designing against hadn't settled. We were pushing a large engineering effort forward against a foundation that was still moving.

Months later, the first joint working session was set up like a classroom — long parallel tables in horizontal rows, all facing the speaker and the screen at the front. I was against the wall in the second-to-last row, far enough back to see the room. Both sides had spent weeks preparing. This was the first time the engineering work would be put up on the screen for everyone to see.

The other team went first. Their lead engineer walked through the early drawings — the process flow diagrams, the basic block layouts, the way the systems were going to fit together. The work was solid. You could see the care in it, the detail, the thinking behind each decision.

My lead process engineer was sitting next to me. After the second or third drawing went up, he leaned over and poked my shoulder.

He didn't have to say what he was thinking. I already knew. We had been in our own design discussions for weeks, working from what we had assumed was a shared set of premises, and the drawings on the screen were not built from those premises. Not slightly off. Built from a different starting point. As the presentation kept going — the equipment list, the sizing assumptions, the way the interfaces had been drawn — the gap got wider, not narrower. This wasn't going to reconcile in the room. It was going to take work, real decisions from people who had been avoiding them, and more time than anyone wanted to spend on a problem that should have been resolved months earlier.

On the surface, the meeting stayed productive. People were professional. The technical questions kept getting asked and answered. But underneath it, both sides were arriving at the same realization at roughly the same time, and nobody was naming it. The problem didn't belong to the room. It belonged somewhere above it, in commercial agreements that hadn't settled, in the points of contact who filtered every cross-organizational message before it reached anyone who could act on it. Raising it directly would mean stepping into territory that hadn't been made safe to enter. So the conversation stayed technical. The discussion stayed productive, on the surface. And the most important issue in the room remained unspoken.

After that meeting, it became clear that neither side's design was as complete as it appeared. Both worked within their own assumptions. But those assumptions did not match. And reconciling them would require changes that were not trivial, enough to affect layout, interfaces, and how the systems would ultimately function together.

All of that effort, on both sides, had been built on a foundation that had never been aligned.

This is how misalignment develops in complex organizations. Not through obvious failure. But through structured silence, through indirect communication that prevents real issues from surfacing cleanly, through assumptions that are never explicitly validated, and through an understanding, shared by many, that something is wrong. And an equally strong understanding that it is not safe to say it out loud.

When the diagnostic reveals divergence — whether through what people say, what the work shows, or what the silence conceals — the issue is not technical. It is leadership. Because leadership is not only about making decisions. It is about creating the conditions where the right problems can be seen early and said without hesitation. And the earlier misalignment is detected, the easier it is to correct.

Alignment Has to Be Confirmed

Years earlier, in a field activity that required a confined space entry, I was responsible on the owner's side for making sure it went as planned. I gathered everyone together — the crew doing the work and my own team — and walked through the hazards and my expectations. When I finished, I asked one of the workers to repeat back what he'd understood. What he repeated back was not what I thought I had communicated. He had filtered the explanation through his own assumptions about the work. In confined space entry, that kind of misunderstanding is the difference between a safe day and a fatal one.

Alignment cannot be assumed. It must be verified.

Alignment Does Not Eliminate Negotiation

Alignment does not mean that everyone immediately agrees with every decision.

Once work begins taking shape, every group involved naturally starts advocating for the interests they are responsible for protecting. Those who will operate the outcome push for reliability and maintainability. Those responsible for the economics push for capital discipline. Those accountable for technical performance push for robust solutions.

None of these perspectives are wrong. The problem arises when leadership has not clearly defined the objective that filters them. Without that filter, every stakeholder pulls in a different direction. With it, those same tensions become productive.

On a brownfield expansion project to increase production capacity, the objective was straightforward: execute at the lowest possible capital cost.

Operations had their own concerns. They wanted additional redundancy in parts of the control system and additional spare components to simplify maintenance. From an operational perspective, those requests made complete sense. But they also increased the capital cost.

Because the objective was clear, the discussion was not about whether operations' concerns were valid. They were. The discussion was about how those concerns fit within the project's objective.

Rather than simply rejecting the request, we worked through it together. We designed the relevant systems so that the additional features could easily be installed later as part of a small follow-on effort owned by operations. The expansion maintained its cost objective. Operations retained the flexibility to add their preferred upgrades later.

No one received exactly what they originally asked for. But the effort remained aligned with its objective, and real concerns were addressed in a practical way.

Alignment does not eliminate negotiation. It makes negotiation productive.

Maintaining Clarity

Establishing clarity is only the beginning. Maintaining it requires something less glamorous but just as important: repetition.

Any complex effort involves many people across multiple functions and sometimes multiple organizations. As work progresses, new people join while others move on. Priorities shift. Pressure builds. And in that environment, clarity fades faster than most leaders expect.

This is how clarity degrades. Not through negligence. Not through conflict. Through the ordinary, relentless pressure of complex work. Every new team member brings their own assumptions. Every significant decision creates an opportunity for the objective to be reinterpreted. Every crisis pulls attention toward the immediate and away from the directional.

The problem with misalignment is rarely the misalignment itself. It is how long it goes undetected. By the time leadership notices that something is off — that the data isn't reconciling, that status reports are telling different stories — the drift has usually been building for weeks, sometimes months. The longer it takes to surface, the more embedded the misalignment has become, and the more expensive it is to correct.

This is also where activity becomes dangerous. It can create the appearance of alignment even when alignment has never been established. People assume they are moving in the same direction because everyone is working hard and discussing the same effort. Working on the same thing, however, does not mean everyone understands it the same way. The pressure to demonstrate progress makes it worse. The organization begins moving before the objective is clear, before the key questions are resolved.

Effective leaders treat clarity not as something established at the beginning of an effort but as something that must be actively protected throughout it. They repeat the objective consistently. Not when it feels necessary, but as a matter of practice. In meetings, in decision discussions, in how they frame trade-offs and evaluate options.

That repetition is not redundancy. It is the work.

And it is the fastest way to build momentum. When teams understand exactly what they are trying to accomplish, decision-making becomes easier. Trade-offs become more obvious. Disagreements get resolved faster because there is a shared reference point for what matters. Momentum builds not because people are working harder, but because they are working toward the same outcome.

Before any complex effort needs execution, it needs clarity. It needs leaders willing to ask the simple question that often reveals the most important problem.

What exactly are we trying to accomplish?

Test for alignment directly. At some point outside the meeting, individually, ask people what the effort is trying to accomplish. Not in front of the group, where answers converge toward whatever was said first. When alignment is real, the wording varies but the core idea holds. When it isn't, you'll hear different versions of success, each reasonable, none the same.

Watch for activity that looks like progress. The tell isn't silence or disengagement. It's motion without convergence. Conversations move from one detail to the next without settling on direction. The group seems close to a decision, then drifts. Everyone leaves busy. Nothing was decided.

Listen for what isn't being said directly. When the real problem sits above the room, in agreements that haven't settled or structures that filter what reaches the people who could act, raising it means stepping into territory that hasn't been made safe. Both sides know. Nobody names it.

Don't assume clarity holds. Every new person joining brings assumptions. Every crisis pulls attention toward the immediate. Clarity doesn't fade because someone decided to change direction. It fades because no one actively protected it. Ask the simple question regularly, not when it feels necessary: *what exactly are we trying to accomplish?*

Chapter 2

The Illusion of Progress

The most dangerous moment in any organization isn't when things are clearly going wrong.

It's when things appear to be going right and aren't.

When things are visibly broken, organizations respond, leaders intervene, and resources are redirected. The problem gets attention proportional to its visibility.

But when an organization is moving confidently in the wrong direction — when activity is high, meetings are full, and everyone appears focused and productive — the problem attracts little to no attention at all. Momentum feels like direction. Busyness feels like purpose. And the gap between what an organization believes it is accomplishing and what it is actually accomplishing can grow, undetected and expensively, for a very long time before it is named.

A startup I was advising had already made a consequential decision without fully realizing it. Their R&D team had developed a version of their core product that worked well enough to move forward — not the final formulation they ultimately wanted, but sufficient to justify building a commercial demonstration facility. So that's what they planned to build.

The logic seemed reasonable on its surface. But underneath it, a contradiction had been embedded into the foundation of everything that followed.

R&D was still working. The better version of the product, the one the company actually intended to bring to market, was still being developed in parallel. The demonstration plant was being designed around the current version. But the real plant, the one that would follow, would need to produce the improved version.

Which meant the organization was investing in a demonstration facility without having resolved the most basic question about it: what exactly was it supposed to demonstrate?

The ability to produce their current product? Their core novel technology operating at scale? Their supply chain? Their ability to start up a first-of-a-kind facility and hit specification?

Each answer leads to a fundamentally different facility. And the organization hadn't converged on any of them.

For some, such as first-of-a-kind companies, that kind of ambiguity is not always fatal. The act of building reveals things the organization couldn't have known otherwise. But in this case, the unresolved question wasn't a gap to be filled through learning. It was a flaw in the foundation.

Compounding this, they had set two objectives for the facility that were fundamentally incompatible. They wanted to build it at the lowest possible capital cost, and they wanted to design it so it could be retrofitted later to accommodate the improved product.

Those two objectives cannot coexist. Every decision that reduces capital cost reduces flexibility. Every design choice that preserves future optionality adds cost. You cannot simultaneously optimize for both.

But the organization had never confronted that contradiction directly. They held both objectives at once and kept moving forward, as if the tension between them would resolve itself somewhere downstream.

It didn't.

I raised this directly, more than once. Each time, the conversation would generate discussion without producing resolution. The question visibly made senior leaders uncomfortable; it would be acknowledged, examined briefly, and then absorbed back into the momentum of everything else that was moving. And the project kept advancing.

At some point the group went to lunch together. On the walk back to the office, the company's engineering manager fell into step beside me and asked what I thought about the company and this effort.

I hesitated. Saying what I was about to say wouldn't just be an observation — it would land as a judgment on how the work was being led, delivered to one of the people most responsible for leading it, in a conversation he had initiated.

And I was on a contract. I could be uninvited from the effort by the end of the week.

I said it anyway.

I told him the company was behaving like an organization that had plenty of time and plenty of money. In reality, it had neither. Every day consumed runway they weren't replacing. Every dollar spent on engineering work built around unresolved questions was a dollar that couldn't be recovered. And they were preparing to enter a significantly more expensive phase of development without first answering the questions that would determine whether that phase should happen at all.

He slowed his pace slightly. He looked thoughtful, almost puzzled, as if he was weighing what I had just said against his own experience.

Then he asked: "Do you really think so? How so?"

I told him what I had seen since I joined. The decisions that had been made without converging on what the facility was actually for. The two incompatible objectives being held at the same time. The conversations that would acknowledge the tension and then absorb it back into momentum. One or two specific examples, nothing dramatic. The things anyone standing close enough could see if they were looking.

He didn't argue with any of it.

He had confused the activity of moving forward with the reality of making progress. And he wasn't alone in it.

This is not a startup problem or an industrial problem. It is what happens in any organization that has built a system designed to reward visible motion. The product team shipping features nobody asked for. The sales leader running plays against a pipeline that hasn't been qualified. The executive team hitting every quarterly milestone while the business underneath them slowly erodes. Each of them feels like they are doing the work. None of them is making progress. And by the time the gap between the two becomes visible, the cost of closing it has already multiplied.

When Momentum Becomes the Objective

In many organizations, the pressure to move forward begins well before the effort itself is ready.

Senior leaders communicate expectations to boards, investors, or internal stakeholders. Those commitments cascade. Vice presidents promise progress to executives. Directors promise progress to vice presidents. At each level, the incentives are understandable. Few people want to be the one reporting that a promised milestone will not be met.

Under those circumstances, advancing appears to be the safest option. A new phase has begun. Progress can be reported. From the outside, everything appears to be moving forward.

But once an effort begins moving, something shifts inside organizations. Momentum starts to create its own justification.

At the beginning, leaders ask fundamental questions. Should we pursue this? Does the business case make sense? What risks do we face?

Once the effort moves into formal development, those conversations change. The organization begins discussing schedules, budgets, milestones, and deliverables. Teams are assigned. Contracts are negotiated.

The effort becomes real. And once it becomes real, stopping it becomes psychologically difficult.

Momentum is not progress. It only feels that way from the inside.

People begin saying things like: "We've already come this far." "We just need to get through the next milestone." "We'll figure that out later."

By then the objective has changed. It is no longer clarity. It is continuation. The effort has to keep moving so no one has to face what isn't working. The shift is never announced. It just becomes the new gravity the whole organization moves under.

The longer that dynamic persists, the harder it becomes to reverse. Each stage creates additional commitments — contracts, deliverables, procurement decisions, staffing plans. Soon the organization finds itself supporting a structure that is increasingly difficult to slow down, even if fundamental questions remain unresolved.

And when unresolved issues begin slowing the effort, organizations often respond by adding more resources. Additional people are assigned. Consultants are hired. New studies are commissioned. But many activities in complex efforts are sequential. Certain questions must be answered before the next layer of work can proceed. Adding more people cannot accelerate work that depends on information that does not yet exist. The result is not faster progress. It is more expensive stagnation.

The Quiet Erosion of the Team

One consequence of pushing momentum ahead of clarity rarely appears in reports.

It shows up inside the team.

Most high-performing teams are composed of capable professionals who spend their careers solving complex problems. Over time they develop a strong sense for when an effort is moving in the right direction and when something is fundamentally misaligned.

When leadership pushes forward despite unresolved questions, the people closest to the work often notice first.

At the beginning, concerns may be raised openly. People ask questions about missing information. They point out practical constraints. They highlight gaps in scope or planning.

But if those signals are repeatedly absorbed into the momentum of the effort, acknowledged but not acted on, something subtle begins to happen inside the team.

The conversation shifts. Instead of raising concerns in formal meetings, people begin discussing them informally, in hallway conversations, over coffee, or in the moments between tasks. The official narrative may still say that progress is being made. But internally, many already sense that something is off.

People convince themselves that someone else must already be aware of the problem. Some sense something is wrong. Others don't. But the people who most need to hear it never do.

Over time the dynamic begins to change behavior. People start asking themselves a simple question: why should I invest effort in work that will likely need to be redone?

This question is rarely spoken aloud, but it changes how people approach their work. Reviews become less rigorous, assumptions are challenged less frequently, and people stop pushing as hard for the best solution because they no longer believe the effort will lead to meaningful progress.

The effort may still appear busy. But the energy behind the work has changed.

Ironically, the very attempt to demonstrate momentum can end up weakening the team's ability to deliver real progress.

When Acceleration Is Strategic

Not all acceleration is misguided. The dynamic this chapter describes is specific, and it's worth separating it from situations where moving quickly is the right call.

There are situations where moving quickly is a deliberate and rational decision. An organization may choose to accelerate in order to reach the market before competitors, secure a strategic position, or respond to rapidly changing conditions. In those cases, leaders knowingly accept additional risk in exchange for strategic advantage.

The difference is awareness, whether leaders know what they're accepting or not.

When acceleration is strategic, leaders understand the risks they are taking. They recognize that unresolved questions still exist and choose to move forward anyway because the potential benefit justifies the uncertainty. Ideally, they also prepare the organization to absorb the consequences if those risks materialize.

The dynamic described in this chapter is different. It occurs when efforts accelerate not because leaders have consciously chosen to accept risk, but because momentum itself has become the objective. The organization begins behaving as if progress must continue simply because progress has already begun.

The Moment Leaders Must Intervene

Experienced leaders eventually learn to recognize a specific signal: progress may be occurring, but decisions don't seem to stick.

The same fundamental questions keep appearing in different forms. Assumptions are repeatedly revisited. Decisions are postponed or sometimes reinterpreted as new information emerges. The effort is moving forward, but its foundation is still shifting.

This is often the moment when leadership matters most.

Someone must recognize that continuing to move forward will not resolve the underlying uncertainty. The effort must slow down long enough to resolve the questions that are driving the confusion.

That decision is uncomfortable. Pausing momentum rarely feels like progress. It may delay milestones, disrupt schedules, or create difficult conversations with stakeholders who expect visible movement.

Yet the most experienced leaders understand that temporary discomfort is far less costly than carrying unresolved uncertainty deeper into the effort. Stopping to validate assumptions or resolve conflicting priorities may feel like a setback in the moment. In reality, it often prevents far larger setbacks later.

The challenge is that many organizations struggle to make this decision. When momentum has already built, slowing down can feel like admitting that something is wrong. As a result, organizations sometimes continue moving forward even when key questions remain unresolved. Everyone hopes that the answers will appear as the effort progresses.

Occasionally they do.

But more often the uncertainty simply becomes embedded deeper, where it becomes harder — and more expensive — to resolve.

Clarity should be improving at the same rate the effort is advancing. When it isn't, when the work moves forward but the fundamental questions remain unresolved, when the same issues keep surfacing in different forms, the effort is not progressing. It is accumulating cost, eventually showing up as a missed market window, a reduced margin, or a write-down that gets explained as something else.

The discipline to pause in that moment, before the cost multiplies, is uncomfortable. It is also the difference between a two-week delay and a two-quarter recovery. The math leaders often get wrong in the moment.

The industrial version of this is expensive because the numbers are large. The version that plays out in reorganizations and strategic pivots is expensive for exactly the same reason. The organization kept moving because moving felt like the safer choice than admitting the ground underneath had shifted. The setting may be different. The bill is not.

Distinguish activity from progress. Clarity should be improving at the same rate the effort is advancing. When the work moves forward but the same fundamental questions keep surfacing in different forms, the effort isn't progressing. It's accumulating cost.

Watch for momentum justifying itself. Listen for the language: "We've already come this far." "We just need to get through the next milestone." "We'll figure that out later." These phrases signal that the objective has silently shifted from clarity to continuation.

Notice where concerns migrate. When concerns move out of formal meetings and into hallway conversations, the team has learned that raising them formally has no effect. That migration is a signal, not background noise.

Resist the reflex to add resources when an effort stalls. Ask first whether the work is waiting on information or on labor. More people applied to an unanswered question produces more expensive stagnation, not faster progress.

Chapter 3

The Consequences Are Yours

You have hired someone capable. You have paid them well. They know what they're doing. And months later, the thing they delivered does not do what you needed it to do.

Was anyone at fault?

Everyone did their job. And you are still the one who has to explain what happened.

In any complex effort, many organizations participate in the work. Engineering firms design systems. Contractors build facilities. Vendors supply specialized technology. Consultants advise. Each group brings expertise. Each group has its own leadership, its own incentives, its own commercial logic.

But none of them own the outcome.

That responsibility belongs to the organization that commissioned the work. The question this chapter is about is whether the owner organization understands what it means to own the consequences.

The distinction sounds obvious. In practice it is a consistently misunderstood responsibility in complex work. When capable firms are hired, it becomes tempting to assume that their capability will carry the effort to the right outcome. They have done this before. They know what they are doing. Let them do it.

That assumption is where many expensive failures begin.

The Safety System

The system already existed. It had been built, installed, and commissioned across a network of industrial terminals — designed by a capable engineering contractor, paid for by an owner who had identified a real and serious safety risk. Static electricity buildup during the loading of flammable product into trucks, which under the wrong conditions could produce an ignition source with catastrophic consequences. The contractor had done exactly what they were asked.

The equipment was installed. The system was running.

And yet, the terminals still had significant safety exposure.

I had been brought in to lead the redesign, and I was going to be overseeing the entire effort: the development work, the rollout across the facilities that were getting the upgraded version, and the first-time installation at the few facilities that hadn't received the original. When I called the first meeting with the contractor's engineers, I walked them through the underlying safety mechanism in detail. I explained how static electricity accumulated, what conditions increased the risk, and precisely how the loading sequence needed to be controlled. Then I described the operating logic.

As I explained it, one of their engineers stopped me.

"This is great," he said. "We didn't get anything like this when we installed the original ones."

For a moment, I didn't respond.

Part of me felt vindicated, not in a personal sense, but in the clarity of what had been missing. Another part of me found it unsettling. Because what he was reacting to wasn't something novel or particularly sophisticated. It was simply a clear definition of the problem. And that hadn't been there the first time.

I glanced around the room. The other engineers weren't surprised, not really. A few nodded slightly, almost as if the gap had just been named out loud for the first time, something they may have already sensed but never fully articulated.

The contractor had the capability. They had always had the capability. What they hadn't had was a clear picture of what the system needed to do. The owner had known the problem — static was building up during loading and creating an explosion risk, and that much was clear and serious. What they hadn't fully understood were the specific mechanisms: the conditions under which the risk increased, the points in the loading sequence where exposure was highest, the precise behavioral controls that would actually reduce it. They believed they understood enough. In good faith, they handed the contractor a problem statement and trusted that engineering capability would do the rest.

That trust wasn't misplaced. The contractor was capable. But capability applied to an incomplete picture produces an incomplete solution. The contractor solved the problem they were given. The problem they were given was incompletely defined, which meant the contractor filled the gaps with their own interpretation — and that work was never theirs to do. It belonged to the organization that would live with the consequences.

Once the engineers understood exactly what the system was meant to accomplish, their work changed. They stopped interpreting vague requirements and started solving the problem directly. They brought useful suggestions. They proposed improvements. But the direction of the effort was no longer ambiguous, because the owner had finally taken the seat the owner was supposed to be sitting in.

I stayed closely involved throughout. I reviewed progress regularly, traveled to the contractor's office, and stayed engaged through the rollout across the facilities. Equipment vendors, programmers, electricians, and operations personnel all ended up integrated into the effort, because integration was part of what the owner's role required.

What the first version had lacked wasn't engineering skill. The contractor had been capable all along. What was missing was someone on the owner's side holding the whole picture, defining what the system had to do, and staying in the work long enough to make sure the definition held.

The Owner Is the Only One Who Can't Leave

You can hire expertise. In fact, you should. Bringing in people who understand the technical domain, who can help define the problem precisely, who can translate business need into engineering requirement — that is exactly the right use of external capability. Understanding itself can be purchased.

What cannot be transferred is the consequences.

When the system falls short, the contractor closes out the contract and moves on to the next engagement. The engineering firm submits the final invoice. The consultant delivers the report. The vendor ships the last piece of equipment. And the organization that commissioned the work lives with what was built, with the gap between what was needed and what was delivered, for years, sometimes decades.

That permanence is what makes ownership non-delegable. Not the paperwork. The permanence.

If anything, expertise doesn't reduce the need for ownership. It amplifies it. The more capable the expert, the faster the effort can move in whatever direction it has been pointed. If the objective and the constraints are not clearly defined, a highly capable organization can develop a technically impressive solution that is nevertheless poorly aligned with what the business actually needed. By the time the misalignment becomes visible, the effort may already be deep enough into execution that correcting it requires redesign, scope reduction, or rework — all of which cost multiples of what early ownership would have cost.

The owner's active involvement is not a sign of distrust toward the experts engaged. It is the mechanism that keeps the effort aimed at the right target, and it is the only thing that reliably does so.

Watching Their Back

Earlier in my career I interviewed for a role at a company whose processes were, by industrial standards, relatively simple. My résumé was heavier on advanced process engineering than the work seemed to require, and I asked them directly.

"Why are you hiring me? You've seen what I've done. Your processes are straightforward. You could find anyone to do this."

The interviewer didn't flinch. He told me that the company had been hiring engineering firms and paying "through the roof" for years, and they were starting to feel taken advantage of. They needed someone on their own team who could watch their back. Someone who could challenge the recommendations coming from outside. Someone who could make sure they weren't overspending by taking someone else's word for it.

That was the job. Not the engineering. The standing to push back.

The company had recognized something most organizations never quite articulate: when the people on your side of the table don't have the standing to question the people on the other side, the other side's logic gradually becomes your logic. Not because anyone is acting in bad faith. Because capability applied without challenge drifts toward whatever the most capable person in the room believes. If that person works for you, that's fine. If the person works for the firm billing you, the drift is exactly as expensive as the hourly rate times the number of decisions nobody questioned.

Most organizations don't hire someone specifically to watch their back. They assume their existing team can do it, and in principle, it should. The problem is that watching your back in a technical domain requires technical standing, and technical standing is exactly what many owner organizations have allowed to atrophy over time, on the theory that expertise can always be hired when it's needed.

Hiring it when you need it is not the same as having it. The gap between the two is where this kind of overspending lives.

Why Ownership Fails

So where does ownership actually break down?

Incomplete problem definition is the most common cause. When the problem has not been clearly defined, technical work begins without the constraints needed to guide it. Teams solve the problem they have in front of them. The problem they have in front of them is the one the owner was able to articulate, which is often not the problem the owner actually needs solved.

In other situations the issue is delegation disguised as leadership. Senior leaders assume that once a capable firm has been hired, the effort will move toward the right outcome on its own. In reality, that assumption transfers decision-making to organizations that do not own the business objective and are not positioned to second-guess it.

In larger efforts another dynamic sometimes appears: internal politics. Complex initiatives create visibility inside organizations. Promotions, influence, and career advancement can become tied to an effort's success. Under those conditions, a handful of people — typically the ones most invested in the outcome for their own advancement — may begin to behave differently. They agree in meetings and then do something different. The version of events they tell in one room is not the version told in the next. They seed their preferred framing with the people they think matter most. Information gets filtered. Concerns get minimized. The effort's actual state becomes harder to see from inside the organization than from outside it.

These dynamics rarely appear in plans or official reports. But when ownership weakens inside the organization, the effort does not stay neutral. It drifts. And the consequences of that drift, whenever they eventually surface, belong to the organization that let it happen.

What Ownership Actually Looks Like

Owning an effort does not mean controlling every decision. It means ensuring that the purpose of the investment stays clear, that the organization doing the work stays aligned with that purpose, and that the people on the owner's side of the table have the standing to hold that line when the effort meets pressure.

It means defining the objective precisely enough that competent execution can be measured against it.

It means staying in the work long enough to catch the places where the definition is being adjusted to fit what's easier.

It means maintaining the internal capability to challenge what you are being told, because what you are being told will otherwise become what you believe.

The next time you commission a solution, ask yourself one question: if the result falls short, who lives with it?

The answer to that question determines who must own the definition. Not the contract. Not the scope. The definition of what the problem actually is, and what the solution actually has to do.

That work cannot be handed off, because the consequences of getting it wrong never are.

Recognize that capability without direction drifts. A capable firm hired to solve a problem will solve the problem in front of them, which may not be the problem you actually need solved. The gap between the two only becomes visible after the work is done and the contractor has moved on. You live with what was built.

Stay in the work long enough to define what the solution has to do. Not the general objective. The specific mechanisms, conditions, and constraints that determine whether the result actually works. If the people doing the work tell you they didn't get that level of definition, the ownership failed before the engineering began.

Maintain the standing to push back. When the people on your side of the table can't question the people on the other side, the other side's logic gradually becomes your logic. Not because anyone is acting in bad faith. Because unchallenged capability drifts toward whatever the most capable person in the room believes. Hiring expertise when you need it is not the same as having it.

Watch for delegation disguised as leadership. The assumption that once a capable firm has been engaged, the effort will move toward the right outcome on its own. That assumption transfers decision-making to organizations that don't own the business objective and aren't positioned to second-guess it.

Chapter 4

Hold the Whole Picture

Owning the effort is necessary. Making the parts of it fit together is a separate job.

That sounds obvious. In practice, it is one of the most consistently underestimated responsibilities in any complex organizational effort and one of the most expensive to neglect.

Any significant effort has parts. Technical workstreams, commercial negotiations, operational planning, finance, construction. Each of them staffed, funded, and producing real work. Each of them led by capable people who know their domain. Even when the owner is engaged, when the definition is clear, when the right people are on the owner's side of the table — none of that guarantees the parts will fit together.

In many organizations, integration is assumed rather than managed. The assumption is that because everyone is working on the same effort, the pieces will naturally assemble into a coherent whole when the time comes. Meetings happen. Updates are shared. Progress is reported across all workstreams.

But reporting progress is not the same as integrating it.

Integration is active work. It requires someone to understand not just what each part of the effort is doing, but how those parts interact, where they depend on each other, and what decisions in one area will constrain or reshape decisions in another. To hold the whole picture. And just as importantly, to communicate it to every part of the effort that needs it.

A company I worked with learned this in one of its most expensive forms. They were building a commercial facility around a complex process that needed three distinct areas of engineering expertise, and their strategy was reasonable on its face: hire three specialized firms, one for each area, and let each deliver a rigorous design package for its assigned scope.

Each firm did exactly that. The deliverables were thorough. The engineering was sound. Each package was a complete, well-developed design for the scope it had been assigned.

The problem became visible when someone added the three estimates together to arrive at a total project cost. The number didn't make sense. Not because anything had been miscalculated, and not because any one firm had done poor work. Each firm had designed a complete, self-sufficient facility for its assigned area — its own utilities, its own support systems, its own boiler, its own everything. Added together, the three estimates reflected three independent plants. The project didn't need three plants. It needed one integrated facility where systems were shared, utilities were sized for the whole, and every design decision was made with the full picture in mind. A single boiler serving the entire facility costs far less than three separate boilers. The same logic applied to virtually every shared system across the project.

By the time I joined the effort, the company already understood that part. What they didn't yet know was how to fix it, or how to move forward from something that had been developed that far in the wrong direction. Beyond the cost, the packages couldn't be used as they were. To move into the next phase, the organization needed one coherent design: a single comprehensive package that could be handed off and built from. What they had instead were three packages that didn't even share the same visual conventions or technical standards. They had been built by different firms, in different ways, for different scopes. They couldn't simply be stapled together.

The assumption underneath all of it was simple and entirely human: the pieces would fit together naturally. Nobody had decided not to integrate. Nobody had weighed the options and chosen fragmentation. They had simply never assigned the work of coherence to anyone.

Fixing it required an experienced project director to diagnose the problem and take it over. It required hiring a fourth engineering firm whose only job was to integrate the three existing packages into a single coherent design. Every layer of the three had to be reconciled, rationalized, and unified before the project could move forward. It added a year and considerable cost. And it was entirely preventable.

The same arithmetic shows up every time work gets parallelized without someone owning the whole. Three product squads each shipping their piece on time and producing a feature set that nobody can use together. Two companies merging with separate HR systems, separate finance systems, separate cultures, and a slide deck that says "integration" without anyone holding the pen. Five consultants delivering five excellent reports that cannot be assembled into a single decision. The work gets done. The pieces don't fit. And the cost of forcing them to fit afterward is always a multiple of the cost of designing them to fit in the first place.

The Integrator Role

Integration is not a task that can be distributed across workstreams and assumed to happen. It is a role. It requires a person or team whose primary responsibility is the coherence of the whole rather than the performance of any individual part.

What does that role actually do?

Some of the work is reactive — noticing when a decision in one workstream has already constrained another, catching cross-workstream assumptions before they harden, asking repeatedly whether the pieces are being developed in ways that will allow them to come together. But the more important work happens earlier, before any of that becomes necessary. It is setting the standard across the board. Establishing the framework the workstreams operate within, so that each one is set up for a successful outcome rather than for the kind of outcome where no individual firm had failed, but together they had not succeeded either. What I have come to call a "failed success".

Each discipline naturally and legitimately optimizes for its own priorities. Without integration, they will pull in different directions. With it, those same priorities become the material from which a coherent whole is built. That coherence has to be someone's job, or it is no one's.

Early Decisions, Late Consequences

There is a structural asymmetry in complex efforts that organizations tend to underestimate until they have experienced it firsthand.

Organizations typically spend fifteen to twenty percent of their total investment on planning and engineering, the phases where the fundamental decisions are made. The remaining seventy-five to eighty percent funds execution: building what was planned. Governance and controls arrive in full force when the full execution budget is approved. By that point the critical decisions — scope, configuration, design basis, key assumptions — have already been made, under a fraction of the scrutiny that will be applied to everything that follows.

The controls that arrive at that stage don't shape the outcome. They enforce it. Whatever was decided in the planning phases, well or poorly, gets executed with discipline and rigor. If something fundamental needs to change after that point, the cost of changing it multiplies dramatically.

This asymmetry is compounded by a subtler problem. Early decisions appear small. The financial expenditures at the planning stage are modest compared to the total investment. Because the cash outlay is limited, the scrutiny applied to the work tends to be limited as well. But the decisions made during these early phases determine much of the effort's entire risk profile. What begins as a small ambiguity in the planning phase can eventually influence hundreds of millions of dollars in capital investment.

The cascading effect compounds this further. In complex efforts, decisions are not independent. They are layered. A choice made in one area influences equipment selection in another, which influences utilities, systems, layouts, and specifications downstream. Each decision becomes embedded across the effort's documentation.

In the early stages, changing a decision is relatively simple. But once the effort progresses, the same change ripples through everything connected to it. What originally looked like a small adjustment can cascade into revisions across the entire effort with each one taking time, adding cost, and introducing new uncertainty into work that had already been considered settled.

This is why the planning phases of any complex effort deserve more scrutiny, not less.

The Vacuum Doesn't Wait

One of the more counterintuitive realities of complex efforts is that delaying a decision does not buy time. It transfers the decision to whoever fills the vacuum first.

The system keeps moving.

When leadership delays a key decision — waiting for better information, more certainty, or a clearer picture — the teams responsible for execution do not stop. They continue working with the information available. They make provisional decisions to keep their workstreams moving. They fill the gaps with assumptions.

Over time, those provisional decisions and assumptions begin forming a structure around the effort. Equipment is specified. Layouts take shape. Procurement discussions begin. Documents are produced that reference and build on the provisional choices made in the absence of clear direction.

Once that structure forms, reversing it becomes increasingly difficult. The decision that was delayed to avoid premature commitment has now become embedded in the effort's foundation and changing it requires unwinding everything built on top of it.

This is one of the more uncomfortable realities of the integrator role. The choice is rarely between deciding now and deciding later with better information. It is more often between deciding now, imperfectly, with the information available, and allowing the system to decide by default, through the accumulation of provisional choices made by teams filling the vacuum.

Default decisions are rarely better than deliberate ones. They are simply less visible.

This does not mean every decision must be made immediately. Some decisions can and should be deferred while more information is gathered. The discipline lies in distinguishing between decisions that can wait and decisions that are already being made whether leadership engages or not. Where possible, early decisions should preserve flexibility, structuring the effort in ways that allow learning without locking the organization into irreversible choices prematurely.

But flexibility is not the same as delay. And the difference between the two is something only the integrator — the person or team holding the whole picture — is positioned to judge.

Because the vacuum doesn't wait for the integrator to arrive.

It fills itself.

The Window Closes Early

The window in which integration can be shaped is narrower than most organizations realize. The critical decisions get made early, often under a fraction of the scrutiny that will be applied to everything that follows. The owner cannot afford to be passive during that window. It closes long before most organizations notice it has.

The question to ask early and repeatedly is whether the pieces of the effort are being developed in isolation or as parts of a coherent whole. If no single person can describe how the workstreams connect, integration is not happening. And by the time that becomes obvious, the cost of recovering from it will far exceed what prevention would have required.

That absence has consequences. And as the previous chapter established, the consequences — as the owner — are yours.

Ask whether anyone owns the whole picture. When work is moving across multiple workstreams and no single person can describe how the pieces connect, integration is not happening. It looks like parallel progress. It is parallel isolation.

Watch for the vacuum filling itself. Delaying a decision does not preserve options. It transfers the decision to whoever fills the gap first. Teams don't stop when leadership delays. They fill gaps with assumptions and provisional choices that become increasingly difficult to reverse.

Apply scrutiny early, not late. The phases where the critical decisions are made consume a fraction of the total budget and receive a fraction of the total oversight. The controls that arrive during execution don't shape the outcome. They enforce whatever was decided earlier, under less scrutiny, when the choices still looked small.

Test whether integration is structural or reactive. If integration conversations are mostly about fixing mismatches between deliverables, the integrator arrived late. The higher-value work is setting standards before conflicts become possible, not reconciling outputs after the work is done.

Part II — The Environment: Truth

When clarity breaks down, truth is next. The environment leaders build determines whether reality reaches the people who need it or stops somewhere along the way.

Chapter 5

You Get the Truth Your Environment Deserves

A CEO I know had a habit that his leadership team found mildly unsettling.

He would show up unannounced.

Not to headquarters. Not to scheduled reviews or formal presentations. He would appear at a plant on a random Tuesday morning, or tell a truck driver that he was riding along for the day. No advance notice. No prepared agenda. No opportunity for anyone to arrange what he was about to see.

He did this deliberately.

Because he had learned something that most leaders eventually discover, if they are paying attention. The version of the organization that shows up for a planned visit is not the same organization that exists the rest of the time.

Plants would become, in his words, unrecognizably clean and orderly the moment a visit was announced. Equipment that had been tagged out for weeks would suddenly be operational. Issues that had been building for weeks would disappear from view.

Everything would look fine.

And that was exactly the problem.

When everything always looks fine, a leader has to start asking uncomfortable questions. Why are customers still complaining if operations are running so well? Why are the numbers falling short if the plants are performing as reported? Why are safety incidents still occurring if the safety budget is being fully spent?

The gap between those questions and their answers is where filtered information lives.

Most leaders don't receive false information. They receive true information that has been carefully selected, softened, and optimistically framed at every level of the organization before it reaches them. Each layer of management adds a little context, a little reassurance, a little optimism. By the time a concern reaches the top, it has been polished enough that it no longer feels urgent, even if the underlying problem is still very much alive.

This is not deception. It is something more insidious, because it is largely invisible and largely unintentional. It is the organization doing what organizations naturally do: presenting their best face upward.

And it happens not because people are dishonest, but because the environment surrounding them has already taught them what is safe to say and what is better left unsaid.

That environment is built by leaders. And it determines more than any reporting system, any dashboard, or any formal review process the quality of information leaders actually receive.

A different CEO, earlier in my career, described this dynamic in terms I have never forgotten. By the time information reached his office, he said, it was like candy sprinkled with powdered sugar.

Everything looked pleasant. Everything sounded manageable. Every report suggested that things were mostly under control. But the information had already been softened to the point where it no longer clearly reflected the reality it was supposed to describe.

Truth is accurate data. And accurate data leads to better decisions. The environment leaders build determines which one they get.

This is not a plant problem. Every leader who has ever received a clean dashboard before an ugly surprise has been on the receiving end of the same dynamic. The board deck that showed healthy metrics right up until the quarter missed. The portfolio review where every project was green until the one that wasn't. The status report that described a risk as "being managed" for the third month in a row. Nobody lied. Each layer simply softened what it passed upward until the signal no longer carried the weight the reality deserved.

The Dashboard Problem

An old friend of mine is a senior executive for a global industrial company. We had worked together years ago and had fallen into the habit of catching up over a beer whenever we ended up in the same city at the same time — nothing formal, just the kind of conversation where you talk about everything, including work, and the work usually gets the most interesting the longer the evening goes on.

We hadn't seen each other in close to five years when we met up one evening. I mentioned, in passing, that I had been spending the last few years advising on major capital projects. That was when he started telling me about his.

It was, at the time, the largest effort his organization had underway. Strategically important. Highly visible. And it was running about thirty percent over budget.

Cost overruns happen. Complex efforts are hard to predict. That part of the story wasn't unusual.

What frustrated him was how predictable the outcome had been.

There had been warning signs throughout. Small signals that something was drifting. Technical concerns. Schedule pressures. Decisions that looked questionable in hindsight.

But those signals rarely surfaced clearly.

He described how the dashboards he received highlighted green indicators prominently. Yellow indicators were visible but less prominent. Red indicators, when they appeared at all, were buried in explanations and qualifications. Technically, the warnings existed but they were diluted enough that no one had to clearly own them.

Later, when the cost overrun became impossible to ignore, everyone could say the indicators had technically been there. But in reality they had been softened so much that they no longer functioned as warnings.

The challenge is rarely the absence of information. The challenge is creating an environment where people are willing to surface that information before it becomes a problem.

What the Opposite Looks Like

Some years back, on a very different kind of project, I saw what the opposite environment looks like.

This one was large and complex, the kind of effort measured in the hundreds of millions of dollars. We were in the conceptual design phase, which in my experience is the phase that makes or breaks an effort. It is where most of the consequential decisions actually get made. A lot of companies treat it as preliminary work. The good ones treat it as the most important phase there is.

The project director understood that. And he had a way of making sure nothing important stayed hidden long enough to hurt us.

Every week, he pulled the entire management team into a meeting built around what he called the trend log. The rule for the trend log was simple, and deliberately loose. If you thought there was at least a 50% chance something might happen — a cost, a delay, a scope change, anything that could move the project — it went in the log. The 50% threshold was a gut feel. It wasn't defensible. It didn't need to be. The whole point was to lower the bar for surfacing things before they hardened into problems.

I raised a few myself. One was a geotechnical study we were planning, where the initial approach was a tabletop assessment based on existing information. It was the lower-cost path, and on paper it was the right starting point. But I had a feeling the existing information might not hold, and that we could end up needing the full field investigation — which would have cost roughly five times as much and added weeks to the schedule.

Nothing had gone wrong. There was no problem to solve. I just had a sense.

That was enough. It went into the log with a rough cost impact and a rough schedule impact, neither of which was particularly accurate. Accuracy wasn't the point. The point was that the possibility was now visible to everyone, and the team could start preparing for it — moving contingency around, adjusting schedule float, laying groundwork with the stakeholders who would need to be involved if the bigger study became necessary.

Every week, we walked through every item on the log. Some got updated with new information. Some moved into the forecast because they had either materialized or become credible enough to be treated as expected outcomes. Some got closed out because the risk had passed or never materialized. Nobody held a closed item against the person who had raised it. Raising something at 50% and being wrong was treated exactly the same as raising something at 50% and being right. Both were the system working as intended.

The result was that very little took the team by surprise. Not because the project was simpler than others I had worked on — it wasn't — but because the friction around information had been deliberately removed. People did not need certainty to be heard. They did not need to wait until a concern was defensible. And they did not need to soften what they saw to make it acceptable to the room.

That environment did not emerge on its own. It reflected the choices of the person leading the effort. Someone who had decided, and shown week after week, that a speculative concern surfaced early was worth far more than a confirmed problem surfaced late.

When Strength Becomes a Barrier to Truth

Silence is not always the result of fear. Sometimes it comes from respect.

The commissioning lead on a large industrial project I worked on years ago was widely known across the organization. Military background, decades of experience, a reputation for getting things done. People respected him. Some feared him. Most did both. When he spoke, people moved. Decisions happened quickly. Progress was visible. On the surface, that looked like strong leadership.

But there was something else underneath it.

The cooling tower became the focus during one particular stretch. It was ready ahead of most of the plant, and there was a push to bring it online quickly because it showed progress. But the plant was still months away from full start-up. Commissioning the tower early meant we would have to maintain it, monitor it, and manage water quality long before it was actually needed. It added cost. It added effort. And it didn't materially change the readiness of the overall system.

That question — why are we doing this now? — never surfaced where it mattered. People saw it. You could hear it in hallway conversations, in small side discussions after meetings. People understood the trade-off. They questioned the timing. They saw the inefficiency. But none of that made it into the room. Not in front of him. Not when the decision was being made.

The cooling tower got commissioned earlier than it needed to be.

Weeks later, during the boiler commissioning, I was running the night shift for a critical procedure. It was a controlled process — pressure building, temperature increasing, operators cycling valves manually to keep everything within safe limits.

At one point, an operator called me over the radio.

"We've got boiler water coming out of the top vent. If anything goes wrong while the guys are up there, someone's getting burned. What do you want to do?"

I had two options.

Follow the procedure exactly, which meant continuing the cycle and accepting the immediate risk to the operator. Or stop the process, lose the night, and wait for direction in the morning. Both of which could have put my job on the line.

There was a third option, one not written in the procedure.

I chose that one.

We rerouted the system temporarily, allowing pressure to relieve through a different path. It carried its own risk. If material carried over, it could damage downstream equipment, millions of dollars' worth.

But it kept people safe.

And it kept the process moving.

By the morning, the procedure was complete.

When the commissioning lead arrived and heard what had happened, the reaction was immediate. We were in a construction trailer with several people present. He was furious. He went through everything that had been done wrong, why the procedure existed, why it shouldn't have been deviated from, why I should have called him.

No one said anything.

When he finished, I answered as calmly as I could.

I told him I should have called him. That part was on me.

I didn't explain my reasoning. That wasn't the conversation the room needed.

But I also told him I wasn't going to apologize for making the decision I believed was right. No one was going to get hurt on my watch. If that decision cost me my job, then so be it.

I meant it. I was early in my career, without the savings to walk away from a job casually, and the reputation I was going to have for the rest of that project — and in that part of the industry — was being written in that trailer, in front of the people watching. I knew that. I also knew that if I softened the answer to keep the job, I would carry the other version of that moment for a lot longer than unemployment would have lasted.

The room stayed quiet.

He told me to go back to the hotel while they decided what to do with me.

As I walked out, people started coming up to me.

"I can't believe you said that."

"I'm glad you did."

Even my own manager — one of the most capable people I've worked with — told me he respected it.

That was the part I didn't understand at first.

Because the decision itself wasn't extraordinary.

What was unusual was saying it out loud.

The same people who had seen the issue with the cooling tower, who had talked about it privately, who had understood it clearly, had not raised it when it mattered.

Not because they didn't care.

But because the environment made it easier to stay silent than to speak.

I came back that night. I kept my job. The decision was ultimately accepted, and privately acknowledged as the right call.

But the dynamic in that room didn't change.

And that stayed with me.

It made me realize that strong leadership, when expressed in a certain way, can unintentionally narrow the space around it. Not through intent or policy. But through presence.

The room had the capability.

It just didn't have the permission.

That dynamic plays out in rooms far beyond industrial projects. The team that privately knows the launch date is unrealistic but won't say it in the review. The direct reports who can describe the CEO's blind spots to each other but never to the CEO. The clinicians who know which protocol is failing patients and keep that conversation in the break room. The permission to say what everyone already sees is not granted by policy. It is granted, or withheld, by the person at the head of the table, usually without realizing they are doing either.

Making It Safe to Speak

Speaking up does not always require confrontation.

In many cases, the most effective way to surface a concern is through a question. Instead of saying "That approach is wrong," you can ask "Would it make sense to look at it this way?" Or: "What happens if we consider this scenario?"

That simple shift changes the dynamic. It allows the concern to surface without forcing the other person into a defensive position. It gives them space to reconsider the problem without losing face.

The same approach works in any organizational setting. It allows truth to enter the conversation without turning it into conflict.

But for that to work consistently, the leader must create an environment where those questions are welcomed. Because if people believe that raising concerns — even respectfully — will create friction, they will stop asking. And once that happens, the organization loses one of its most valuable assets: the ability to see problems early.

That ability is not a function of how smart the people are. It is a function of whether the environment makes it safe for smart people to say what they actually see.

That environment is built one response at a time. Every time a leader reacts to a concern with curiosity rather than defensiveness, the environment becomes slightly safer. Every time a difficult question is welcomed rather than dismissed, the signal reaches everyone watching.

And in organizations, everyone is always watching.

The next time someone brings you an uncomfortable piece of information, notice your own reaction before you respond. That reaction, visible to everyone in the room, is building the environment whether you intend it to or not.

Notice the gap between reported performance and lived reality. Customers still complaining when operations are "running well." Numbers falling short when plants are "performing as reported." Nobody is lying. Each layer softens what it passes upward until the signal no longer carries the weight the reality deserves.

Watch what happens to warnings in your reporting. Green indicators highlighted prominently, red buried in explanations and qualifications. A risk described as "being managed" for months in a row. Warnings that technically exist but have been diluted enough that no one has to clearly own them.

Lower the threshold for raising concerns. Whether people need certainty before they can be heard, or whether they can speak from a sense, determines how early your organization sees problems. Treat a concern raised early and proven wrong exactly the same as one proven right. Both are the system working.

Notice your own reaction before you respond. The next time someone brings uncomfortable information, watch what you do with it before you answer. That reaction, visible to everyone in the room, is building the environment whether you intend it to or not.

Chapter 6

Fostering Productive Disagreement

When disagreement surfaces in a room, most leaders feel an instinct to manage it.

Not to engage with it. To manage it. To smooth the tension before it escalates. To redirect the conversation toward safer ground. To protect relationships, preserve momentum, and avoid the kind of moment that might be difficult to walk back.

That instinct is understandable. Disagreement is uncomfortable. Strong opinions create friction. And leaders who have watched a productive discussion tip into something personal know that the line between debate and conflict can feel thin in the moment.

But that instinct, however well-intentioned, extracts a cost that rarely shows up in the meeting where it originates.

It shows up later. In decisions that were never properly challenged. In assumptions that moved through the organization unchallenged because the room felt too uncomfortable to question them. In solutions that failed in practice because the people who could see the flaw decided, based on past experience, that raising it wasn't worth the friction.

The leader who smooths over disagreement believes they are protecting the team. In most cases they are protecting themselves from an uncomfortable moment and handing the team a far more expensive problem downstream.

Silence Is a Warning Sign

When disagreement disappears from a room, leaders often interpret it as a sign that the team is aligned.

More often, it is a sign that something has gone wrong.

Silence is not agreement. Silence is frequently unresolved tension that has not yet surfaced. And unresolved tension does not disappear. It accumulates until it eventually surfaces in a form that is far more expensive to address.

One of the most revealing moments in any meeting occurs when a difficult issue is placed on the table. The room is filled with experienced professionals who understand the implications. And yet the room becomes quiet.

In healthy environments that rarely happens. People who spend their careers solving difficult problems tend to have strong opinions about difficult problems. They notice risks. They see constraints. They understand trade-offs.

When those voices disappear, something else is happening. Sometimes people have concluded that raising the concern will not change the outcome. Sometimes they sense that the decision has already been made. Whatever the reason, silence in those moments should concern any leader.

The issues hidden behind that silence will eventually emerge, when the cost of addressing them is much higher than it would have been if they had surfaced in the room.

What Productive Disagreement Looks Like

One of the most effective team environments I ever worked in was one that my former boss once described, half jokingly, as being made up entirely of type-A personalities.

He wasn't wrong.

The group included strong professionals across multiple disciplines who were not shy about defending their ideas. But what made the team work was not personality. It was mutual respect.

People challenged each other constantly, sometimes aggressively. But everyone understood that the disagreement was about solving the problem, not about attacking the person proposing the idea. That distinction allowed the team to push hard on difficult issues without damaging relationships. The arguments never broke the team. They strengthened it.

The organization had experienced an explosion during a truck loading operation. Fortunately, no one was seriously injured, but the implications were significant. This organization operated terminals across the country that loaded flammable chemicals into trucks every day. Even a minor explosion meant something in the system had to change immediately.

A small team spent roughly a week analyzing the loading process and developing a new procedure designed to prevent the incident from happening again. Once the proposal was ready, we presented it to a broader group for review.

The meeting took place on a Saturday.

After a full week of long days, we were all back in a conference room with senior leadership. The director of engineering was present, along with the engineering team I had been asked to lead. The vice president of operations sat at the table. Several regional operations directors participated, some in person and others remotely. Consultants who had been brought in for specific technical aspects were also involved.

No one in that room was there casually.

And the discussion quickly became intense.

At times the conversation was light. There was laughter. But those moments didn't last long.

One of the operations directors leaned back and said:

"I've been doing this for thirty years. I've never seen this happen."

I responded more directly than I probably should have:

"It doesn't happen — until it does. And when it does, it's already too late."

Another followed almost immediately:

"If we implement this the way you're suggesting, we're going to slow production down significantly."

Then the real concern surfaced:

"And when that happens, we're the ones who answer for it. Not you."

That was the moment the tone changed. No one was arguing that the incident didn't matter. Everyone agreed it couldn't happen again. The question was how far the organization was willing to go, and who would carry the consequences.

That didn't resolve anything. But it made the reality harder to dismiss.

The conversation escalated. Voices overlapped. People interrupted each other. Arguments started stacking — safety versus production, probability versus consequence, theory versus reality.

At one point, one of the directors stood up, leaned forward, and struck the table with his hand.

"You need to understand, this is not theoretical for us."

For a moment, the room went quiet.

Then the discussion resumed, louder than before.

From the outside, someone observing that meeting might have assumed the conversation had become unproductive. In reality, the opposite was happening.

During the discussion, a critical assumption began to unravel.

The procedure we had designed relied on a piece of equipment that we believed trucks would have available during loading. On paper, the solution made sense. It was clean. It addressed the failure mode directly.

But the operations leaders began pushing back.

"Not every truck has that."

Another added:

"And even when they do, you can't count on it working the same way every time."

The engineers were seeing it at the same time. The proposal wasn't wrong. It just wasn't reliable enough.

I had walked in with a proposal I believed in. By this point, it was clear it wasn't going to survive the room. That wasn't easy to accept. But I wasn't going to let it get in the way of a better answer.

Without that discussion, it would have been approved. It would have been implemented. And it would have failed the first time it encountered the reality of the field.

The energy in the room shifted. The argument wasn't about defending positions anymore. It became about solving the problem within the constraints that had just been made visible.

The vice president called for a short break.

Outside the room, the tone changed. People started talking differently. Not defending ideas but explaining concerns. Coming up with alternatives. Connecting pieces that hadn't fully surfaced in the formal discussion.

By the time we came back, the same directors who had pushed back hardest began offering solutions.

"If we can't rely on that equipment, then we need something that works regardless of the truck configuration."

Another added:

"Then we phase it. Fix the highest-risk factors first and deal with the rest in stages."

Now the discussion was moving. Not cleanly, but constructively.

The final approach achieved the same safety objective, but it removed reliance on equipment that trucks might not have or that might not perform reliably. The solution worked across the entire fleet without exception.

It wasn't the solution we had walked in with.

It was better.

The disagreement had not slowed the team down. It had prevented a flawed solution from being implemented.

What I remember most about that meeting was not the argument. It was what happened afterward.

That evening, several of us went out for dinner together. The atmosphere was relaxed. The conversation had nothing to do with the heated discussion earlier in the day. No one carried the disagreement with them. No one interpreted the debate as personal.

The friction had been necessary.

And it had worked.

Every strong team I have seen, inside industry and outside it, has some version of that meeting in its history. The product review where someone finally said the feature didn't work. The strategy offsite where the CFO pushed back hard enough that the plan actually changed. The design critique that felt uncomfortable while it was happening and produced something better because of it. The friction is not a side effect of a healthy team. It is one of the things that makes it healthy.

When the Right Answer Arrives Too Early

There were many meetings, early in my career, where I could see the solution clearly. The problem was well understood. The constraints were visible. The path forward seemed obvious.

So I would say it. Early in the discussion.

And then something strange would happen. Nothing.

The conversation would continue as if the idea had never been mentioned. People would keep debating. They would explore alternatives. They would go back and forth on details that, from my perspective, had already been resolved.

And then, almost predictably, someone else would say it. Sometimes in different words. Sometimes almost verbatim. And suddenly, the room would align.

For a long time, I saw that as inefficiency — and it frustrated me every time. Eventually, I realized it was something else.

People do not engage with solutions the same way they engage with their own thinking. Before someone is ready to accept an idea, they need to work through the problem themselves. They need to test their assumptions. They need to feel that they have been heard.

Only then do they become open to other viewpoints.

It changed how I approached every discussion after that. Sometimes what looks like wasted time is actually part of the process. The discussion is not only about finding the answer. It is about creating the conditions for the answer to be accepted.

Over time, I adjusted. Instead of presenting the solution immediately, I would listen. I would let the discussion unfold. And then, once the room had fully engaged with the problem, I would introduce the idea — if it hadn't already been raised by someone else. The outcome was different. The timing made the difference.

The dynamic is even more pronounced for leaders. When a leader presents a solution too early, they can unintentionally shut down the very debate they are trying to encourage. And unlike a peer doing the same, the authority behind the position makes it harder for others to push back, even when they should. By holding back initially, leaders create space for the team to think and increase the likelihood that the final decision reflects the full intelligence of the group.

When Authority Shuts Down the Room

Early in my career, I had been tasked with developing and delivering training to operators preparing to start up a new facility. My boss at the time sat in the room during the session.

At one point I was explaining how a particular unit worked in this specific plant. The design had some differences compared to other facilities. One detail in particular mattered — a specific material in the system was there to remove moisture from the stream before it reached the next stage of separation.

As I explained it, my boss interrupted. He disagreed with the explanation and stated that the material served a different purpose.

I had a choice. I could challenge him directly, in front of the entire group. Or I could handle it differently.

I chose to step back and respectfully suggest that we revisit the point later.

His response was immediate. He looked at me the way someone looks at a subordinate who has just challenged something that wasn't meant to be challenged — as if the correction wasn't about the material at all, but about restoring the proper order of things.

"No, there's nothing to discuss."

The words hit before I fully processed them. My heartbeat rose. My palms started to sweat. Part anger, part embarrassment, part something harder to name. The kind of moment where you become suddenly and acutely aware of every face in the room. Some people looked at me. Others looked away, the way people do when they have just witnessed something they weren't supposed to see and don't know where to put it. I remember thinking that whatever credibility I had walked in with had just been taken from me, publicly, and that there was nothing I could do about it except stand there and absorb it.

I took a breath and carried on. It was the only option.

And the conversation moved on.

From that point forward, the dynamic in the room changed. What had been a training session became something else. I finished the session, but the energy was gone.

Later that day, we discussed it privately. He had gone back and reviewed the material. And he acknowledged that I was right.

But that correction never made its way back to the room.

The operators who had been present never saw the discussion resolved. And more importantly, they saw how quickly a discussion could be shut down. That matters. Because moments like that shape how people behave in future conversations. The next time a question arises, people remember whether speaking up led to discussion or whether it was dismissed.

Leaders do not need to intend that outcome for it to happen. It can occur in a single moment. A single response. A single decision to close a discussion instead of exploring it.

The team learns from the moment, not from the intention behind it.

The Leader's Role

Creating an environment where debate improves decisions is not passive.

When someone challenges an idea, the leader's response matters. If the response is defensive, the discussion narrows immediately. If the response is curious, the discussion opens. When the conversation starts drifting toward personalities, the leader has to bring it back to the problem. When one voice begins to dominate, the leader has to create space for others.

Sometimes that is as simple as asking: "What are we missing?" Or: "Does anyone see this differently?"

Those questions do more than gather input. They signal that disagreement is expected.

The people I argued with most intensely on that safety project are the ones I still talk to today. The ones I trust. The ones I would call when I need an honest opinion on something that matters.

Those relationships were built not by avoiding friction. But by working through it.

That is what productive disagreement produces, when leaders hold the space for it rather than smooth it away. Not just better decisions in the moment. But stronger teams over time.

The most dangerous moment in any discussion is when a leader feels the urge to resolve it. That urge feels like leadership. Often, it is the opposite. The room may need the discomfort more than it needs the resolution because the discomfort is where the best thinking happens. Holding that space longer than feels natural is the discipline. The decisions that come out of it will be worth the wait.

Treat silence as a signal, not as agreement. When experienced professionals who normally notice risks and understand trade-offs go quiet, something is being withheld. The issues behind that silence will emerge later, at higher cost.

Let the discussion do its work before resolving it. The most dangerous moment is when a leader feels the urge to end the disagreement. That urge feels like leadership. Often it's the opposite. The room may need the discomfort more than the resolution.

Recognize that timing matters more than being right. A solution offered too early — especially by the leader — can shut down the thinking it was meant to encourage. The discussion isn't only about finding the answer. It's also about creating the conditions for the answer to be accepted.

Fix public closures publicly. When a discussion gets shut down in front of the group, the team learns from the moment, not from the intention behind it. A private correction afterward doesn't undo what the room witnessed.

Chapter 7

When the Right Hand Doesn't Know

There is a version of every important conversation that never happens.

It gets replaced by an email that sits in someone's inbox for three days. Or a question that waits for the next scheduled meeting. Or a concern that gets documented in a report that the right person never quite reads carefully enough.

The information exists. It just never reaches the person who needs it, in the form they need it, at the moment it would still be cheap to act on.

That gap, between information that exists somewhere in an organization and information that is actually shared across it, is one of the most consistent and least dramatic sources of organizational failure. It doesn't announce itself. It accumulates. And by the time it becomes visible, the cost of addressing it is almost always higher than the cost of having prevented it.

Every organization experiences this. A sales team commits to a timeline that engineering hasn't validated. A product decision gets made without the people who will implement it in the room. A regulatory requirement changes and the team working from the old assumption doesn't find out until the work is already done. The information existed. It just didn't travel.

One of the most dangerous versions of this I ever caught personally started with an email about environmental emissions numbers.

It was around 9:30 a.m. when I opened her email.

Two short paragraphs, a question about the emissions numbers in the permit application we had already submitted to the state.

I pulled up the file to double-check before replying. Then I opened the latest design data.

The numbers didn't match.

Not slightly. Enough that it mattered.

I sat there for a second and went back through the last few weeks in my head. The design had been evolving with updates and adjustments, nothing unusual. No single change that would have triggered a meeting.

The permit application had gone in earlier, based on what we knew at the time.

Since then, the design had moved gradually. And no one had connected the two.

The environmental team was working from the permit application they had filed. We were working from the updated design. Both were correct, based on what each group knew.

They just weren't the same.

Two groups. Same project. Different numbers.

And no one had flagged it.

I stood up and walked upstairs.

Her door was open. She looked up as I knocked.

"Hey, what's up?"

"I just saw your email about the permit," I said. "Do you have a few minutes? I think something's off."

"Sure."

I pulled up both sets of numbers.

"These are the ones in the permit application," I said.

She nodded.

"And these are the current design numbers."

She leaned forward. "When did that change?"

"Over the last few weeks," I said. "I don't think it made its way back to you."

She looked at the screen again. Something crossed her expression. Then she looked back at me.

"If we build it like this," she said, "the stack test will fail."

Not maybe. Not potentially. Will.

I knew what that meant.

The state would test the facility against the numbers in the permit, not against the design. If they didn't line up, they could shut the operation down until they did.

This wasn't paperwork.

This was a shutdown risk.

"How long do we have to fix it?" I asked.

She clicked through the timeline.

"If we submit a revision this week, we're fine," she said. "If we wait, it starts affecting construction."

"Okay," I said. "Tell me exactly what you need from me."

"I need confirmed numbers," she said. "Not estimates. And I need them by tomorrow."

"Done."

That conversation took about twenty minutes.

The next day, she submitted the revision. Construction stayed on schedule. Months later, when the system was tested, it passed.

Nothing dramatic happened.

Because we caught it when it was still cheap to fix.

That is what information flow actually looks like when it works. Not a sophisticated system. Not a formal process. A person walking upstairs and having a direct conversation with the colleague who needed to know. The environment allowed it, the relationship supported it, and the distance between the problem and the fix was about thirty feet of hallway and twenty minutes of attention.

Important information loses something every time it gets handed off to a channel instead of a person. And the moments where a conversation would have been cheaper than a process are almost always invisible until the process fails.

The harder problem is when the structure of the organization itself prevents it from traveling at all.

A particular form of this shows up in the way organizations handle procurement.

On the surface, procurement is a routine function. Requisitions are submitted, vendors are contacted, negotiations take place, and equipment is purchased. But in practice, very little about it is routine, especially for large, specialized equipment that carries its own constraints, risks, and timeline.

In one instance, a facility needed to procure a major piece of equipment. It wasn't a long, multi-year project. It was a smaller effort, moving quickly, with limited room for delay. The project manager had done what project managers are expected to do. He worked backward from the installation date, coordinated timelines with procurement, and built a schedule that aligned construction, delivery, and installation.

Everything was in motion. Crews were mobilized. Site work had begun. Foundations were being prepared. The assumption, based on prior coordination, was that the purchase order for the equipment would be issued on time.

Then a week passed. No purchase order.

At first, it didn't seem critical. But when the project manager followed up, the answer he received wasn't about timing. It was about price.

"We're still negotiating," procurement said. "We're close to getting a better deal."

The project manager pushed back. "We're already mobilized. The schedule assumes that equipment is in process. If this slips, everything behind it slips."

Procurement didn't see it that way. "We're saving a significant amount here. It's worth taking a little more time."

The problem was that they were optimizing for different outcomes. Procurement was measured on cost savings alone. The project manager was measured on schedule and execution. Both were doing exactly what they were expected to do.

And that was precisely the issue.

As the delay extended, the consequences became visible. The crews on site continued their work, moving toward a point where they would be ready for installation — with nothing to install.

The conversation grew more direct.

"We're losing more waiting than you'll ever save on this purchase."

The response was just as firm. "My responsibility is to secure the best price."

And there it was.

Not disagreement. Separation.

They weren't working together to achieve a shared objective. They were working in parallel, each optimizing for a different measure of success, inside the same organization.

Eventually, the issue was escalated. Adjustments were made. The equipment was ordered. But the delay introduced additional cost. The schedule slipped. The very savings procurement had worked to secure were offset, then exceeded, by the cost of waiting.

No one had made a mistake. No one had failed to do their job.

And the company still lost.

Because the system had allowed two parts of the same organization to operate without a shared understanding of what actually mattered. Someone was accountable for the total — on paper. But no single person was positioned to see both things happening at once, which meant the accountability existed without the visibility to act on it.

Process Should Enable Conversation, Not Replace It

There is a natural tension in large organizations between structure and speed. Formal processes ensure that decisions are documented, reviewed, and aligned with broader requirements. Those functions are real and they matter. But the same processes, applied without judgment, can slow down the interaction that organizations depend on for real-time learning.

If every question must follow a formal path, people begin to ask fewer questions. If every interaction requires coordination, communication becomes selective. And when communication becomes selective, important information gets delayed, sometimes past the point where it would have been cheap to act on.

A question resolved in a five-minute conversation stays resolved. The same question routed through formal channels for a week can reshape every decision made in the meantime.

The goal is not to eliminate structure. It is to make sure structure does not replace conversation.

Breaking Silos Is a Leadership Decision

Silos are not created by org charts. They are created by behavior, and behavior follows what leaders model and tolerate.

Do leaders encourage direct communication across functions? Do they make it acceptable for people to bypass formal channels when speed matters? Do they bring the right people into conversations early, before the decisions have hardened? The best ones go further — they create legitimate pathways for informal communication, so that a direct conversation across functions doesn't feel like bypassing the system but using it as intended.

People pay attention to those signals. If leaders make it easy to collaborate, people will collaborate. If leaders make it difficult, people will stay within their lanes and assume someone else is holding the broader picture.

The morning I walked upstairs and knocked on that door was not a heroic act. It was a five-minute decision to have a conversation instead of sending an email.

But that kind of decision, made consistently, across an organization, at every level, is what separates teams that catch problems early from teams that discover them late.

The next time you identify something that another team needs to know, notice what you do with it. If your first instinct is to document it and wait for the next meeting, ask yourself what that delay will cost and whether a twenty-minute conversation would have been cheaper.

Most of the time, it is.

Watch for information that exists but doesn't travel. The gap between information that exists somewhere in the organization and information that reaches the person who needs it at the moment it would still be cheap to act on. When a discrepancy surfaces, go directly to the person who needs to know. Don't route it through a channel and wait.

Look for separation, not disagreement. Two functions can operate in parallel, each optimizing for a different measure of success, with no integration point. The tell is not that they're arguing about the right course of action. It's that they're not talking to each other about it at all.

Audit whether process is enabling conversation or replacing it. When every question must follow a formal path, people ask fewer questions. A question resolved in a five-minute conversation stays resolved. The same question routed through formal channels for a week reshapes every decision made in the meantime.

Notice your first instinct when you spot something another team needs. If it's to document it and wait for the next meeting, ask what that delay will cost and whether a direct conversation would have been cheaper.

Part III — The Threats

With clarity weakened and truth compromised, governance, process, and culture begin breaking down in their own way.

Chapter 8

When Authority Becomes Ambiguous

Every organization, at some point, faces a decision that nobody wants to own.

The stakes are visible. The consequences of getting it wrong are real. And the people in the room — capable, experienced, well-intentioned — find reasons not to be the one who makes the call.

Sometimes it's explicit. "I'm not making that decision." — is at least honest.

More often it's quieter than that. The decision doesn't get refused; it gets deferred. More analysis is requested. Additional stakeholders are identified who should probably be consulted. The meeting ends with a follow-up scheduled. And at the next meeting, the same dynamic plays out again.

From the outside, it looks like diligence. Inside the room, everyone knows it's something else.

And the cost of avoidance is rarely zero. While a decision is being deferred, the organization keeps moving. Work proceeds on assumptions. Resources get committed. By the time the avoided decision finally arrives, or gets forced by circumstances, the organization has already traveled in a direction nobody explicitly chose. And the decision now carries the weight of everything built on top of the assumptions that filled the vacuum.

Caution, in this sense, does not reduce risk. It relocates it, from the person who should have decided to the organization that has to live with the default.

This is not unusual human behavior. Making a high-stakes call and having it go wrong is career-limiting in many organizations. Making no call, or ensuring that the call gets diffused across enough people that no single person can be held responsible, is safer. The incentive to protect oneself from visible failure is real and understandable.

What makes it organizationally destructive is when the structure meant to manage it — governance — either doesn't exist, doesn't function, or gets abandoned.

Governance is more than an administrative formality. It is the mechanism through which organizations make decisions clearly, consistently, and with accountability attached. It defines who has authority to decide, how competing priorities get resolved, and what happens when the answer isn't obvious.

When governance works, decisions get made. They may not be perfect. But they are stable and the organization can move forward with confidence that the ground beneath it isn't shifting.

When governance breaks down, decisions become harder to trace. Authority becomes ambiguous. And the organization begins responding less to its stated objectives and more to whatever forces happen to be dominant in any given moment.

When Influence Moves Outside the Structure

On one significant effort, the organization I was working for had engaged an external engineering firm to support the work. We had built what appeared to be a clear formal structure to manage it.

On paper, the structure looked solid. Decision authority was documented. Reporting lines were defined. The engineering manager within our organization was responsible for directing the work, and while the contractor interacted with the broader team, formal instructions flowed through that manager.

But what looked clear on paper began to behave very differently in practice.

Before moving forward on anything consequential, people would pause. Not to think through the decision more carefully. But to navigate the politics around it. Who needed to be involved? Had this already been aligned with the right people? Might it be challenged later by someone outside the immediate discussion?

The team had stopped trusting that the formal process would protect them. They were managing around it instead.

What had happened was that influence had begun moving outside the formal structure. Senior individuals from the participating organizations had started intervening directly, not through the established governance channels, but through side conversations, informal directives, and last-minute changes to decisions that had already been formally reviewed and approved.

At first, the structure still appeared to be working.

In practice, it began to behave differently. The pattern repeated again and again. We would issue direction to the engineering contractor. They would develop the design accordingly, and the work would move forward as expected. Then we would enter a review meeting, present the output, and the project director would step in with some version of: "No, this won't work. We need to change it." The explanation rarely came from the work itself. It came in the form of "someone raised concerns" — and that "someone" wasn't part of the working structure. They hadn't been involved in the prior discussions or the analysis. But they had influence, and their input carried weight.

The first few instances felt manageable. Adjustments happen. Projects evolve.

But it kept repeating. Direction would be given. Work would be completed. And then, in a separate conversation that no one in the room had been part of, the decision would be undone.

As a result, the dynamic began shifting.

The engineering contractor noticed it before anyone said it explicitly. They were being asked to follow one set of instructions, only to see those instructions overridden by people outside the defined structure.

Soon after, those same individuals began appearing in meetings they had not been part of before. Review sessions that had once been focused became crowded. Opinions entered late in the process, often without context but with enough authority to redirect the outcome.

From that point forward, the behavior shifted. Not openly. But noticeably.

The contractor would acknowledge direction, then hesitate. Wait. Test whether the instruction would hold. In some cases, they began incorporating feedback from these informal actors before formal approval was even given.

They had learned which process actually mattered. And it wasn't the one on paper.

The question was no longer "What is the right answer?" It became: "Which answer will survive all the conversations we're not part of?"

The structure had not been removed. It had been bypassed.

Over time, the teams doing the technical work learned to operate accordingly. The effect on the work was corrosive. Teams stopped asking what the best answer was and started asking what answer would survive. The effort was no longer being optimized. It was being negotiated.

When authority becomes ambiguous, teams stop asking what the best answer is and start asking whose approval the answer will need to survive. The result is not necessarily bad intent. It is effort pointed toward navigating the politics around the decision rather than making it.

When Breaking the Structure Is Right

This chapter is not an argument for governance rigidity.

There are situations where the formal decision-making structure should be overridden, where circumstances demand that someone act outside the established process.

The disaster on the Piper Alpha oil platform in 1988 stands as one of the most devastating illustrations of what happens when that clarity is absent. A series of decisions — some made, many avoided — allowed a catastrophic fire and explosion to unfold that killed 167 people. What stood out to me about the Piper Alpha event was the difficulty individuals in positions of responsibility had in overriding a process that was clearly failing, in part because the authority to do so was not clearly established.

One lesson I take from Piper Alpha is not that governance should be ignored when it becomes inconvenient. It is that governance structures must include clarity about when and how they can be appropriately overridden, and that the absence of that clarity creates its own catastrophic risk.

A decision being revisited because new consequential information has emerged is not the same as a decision being reversed because a new voice with seniority has entered the conversation.

The first is governance working. When someone identifies a risk that genuinely changes the analysis, revisiting the decision is exactly what a healthy process should do.

The second is governance failing. When a decision gets reversed not because the analysis changed but because someone with organizational power disagreed outside the established process, the structure is being undermined rather than used.

Leaders who cannot distinguish between the two will either defend flawed decisions in the name of process or allow the process to be casually bypassed in the name of seniority. Neither produces good outcomes.

What Consistent Governance Requires

Good governance does not require perfect decisions. It requires consistent ones.

When authority is clear and the decision-making process is respected, even imperfect decisions create forward momentum. The organization knows how choices were made, who made them, and what criteria guided them. When new information emerges, the process can accommodate it. When a decision proves wrong, accountability can be traced.

When governance is inconsistent — when authority is ambiguous, when informal influence operates alongside formal structure, when decisions recycle because nobody is willing to own them — the organization loses something more fundamental than any single decision.

It loses the ability to trust its own process.

And once that trust erodes, people stop investing in the formal process because they have learned it doesn't determine outcomes. They start investing in informal influence instead, navigating politics, positioning themselves to be in the right conversations rather than making the right arguments.

The effort stops being optimized. It starts being survived.

A process can be imperfect and still work. But it must be either honored or improved. It cannot be selectively bypassed and still be expected to carry weight.

Every large organization has some version of this. The strategy that says one thing and the real strategy that is reconstructed each week from who the CEO had lunch with. The decision committee that meets on Thursday and is overturned on Friday by a phone call nobody was on. The promotion process everyone officially respects and nobody believes. When people stop trusting that the visible process is the real process, they don't revolt. They adapt. They start investing their energy in the conversations they are not supposed to need to have, and the organization pays the cost of that adaptation in every decision that follows.

If you lead an effort and cannot clearly answer who has authority to make a specific decision, and whether that authority will hold once the decision is made, the governance structure is not functioning. It does not matter what the org chart says. It matters what actually happens when a hard call needs to be made.

Test that before it tests you.

Recognize avoidance dressed as diligence. More analysis, more stakeholders, follow-up meetings where the same dynamic replays. The decision doesn't get refused. It gets deferred. While it's deferred, the organization keeps moving on assumptions nobody explicitly chose. Caution does not reduce risk. It relocates it.

Watch for the shadow structure. When people pause before a consequential decision, not to think through it but to navigate who needs to be involved and whether it might be challenged later, the formal structure has been bypassed. The question has shifted from "What is the right answer?" to "Which answer will survive?"

Test your governance before circumstances test it. If you lead an effort and cannot clearly answer who has authority to make a specific decision and whether that authority will hold, the governance structure is not functioning. It doesn't matter what the org chart says.

Distinguish new information from new seniority. A decision revisited because consequential new information has emerged is governance working. A decision reversed because a new voice with seniority entered the conversation is governance failing.

Chapter 9

When the Process Stops Being Real

Most professionals have experienced the meeting that could have been an email. That kind of meeting is frustrating. It wastes time. It signals poor planning or weak facilitation.

But it is not what this chapter is about.

The meetings described here are different and, in some ways, more difficult to name, because the problem isn't inefficiency. It is the meeting where the discussion continues but the decisions don't arrive. Where the conversation circles the same territory without converging. Where people present their analysis, answer the questions, address the objections, and leave the room with the unsettling sense that nothing actually happened.

Not because the meeting was poorly run. But because the meeting was never designed to produce an outcome.

The feeling in the room is distinctive. There is a mix of frustration and awkwardness, a kind of low-grade boredom that sets in when people realize the wheels are spinning but the vehicle isn't moving. Experienced professionals usually sense it before they can name it. Look around that room and you will often see the signal clearly: people are looking down at phones, at laptops, because whatever is on those screens has become more interesting than what is happening in the conversation. That is not a technology problem. It is a meeting problem.

It is a useful self-check for any leader. If you look around the room and the screens are winning, the instinct is to call it an efficiency problem. Sometimes it is. But sometimes it is something else: a signal that the people in the room have already sensed what this chapter describes.

Because the real decisions, whatever they are, are happening somewhere else.

The Meeting That Was Never Real

The consolidation effort in Mexico was supposed to combine two facilities into a single new site. I was running the early stages — meeting partners, visiting sites, negotiating conditions that could support the consolidation. I was on planes almost every week.

But nothing was ever formalized. No agreements. No contracts. Nothing that actually moved the work forward in a durable way.

Every time I got close to something tangible, it would shift.

I would come back, sit across from the VP, walk him through the progress, answer his questions, outline next steps. He would engage seriously, ask thoughtful questions, challenge assumptions, follow the logic, and then redirect me.

Not to continue. To pursue something adjacent. Something related enough to feel productive, but far enough to put everything else on hold.

That pattern repeated. Again and again.

It wasn't that the work lacked effort. It lacked commitment. Nothing was allowed to land.

Only later did the explanation emerge. The organization was in the middle of an acquisition process that could not be disclosed to the team. Senior leadership already knew that the consolidation effort would not proceed but they were unable to reveal that information.

So the team continued working. Meetings continued. Assignments continued. But the outcome had already been decided.

When the VP finally sat us down and explained what had been happening, the reasoning was simple. The information about the acquisition could not be shared, so the team had to remain occupied until the situation became clear.

From a procedural standpoint, that explanation was understandable. From the perspective of the people doing the work, the damage wasn't operational.

It was trust.

I had spent months traveling back and forth. I had been in rooms with people whose time I had asked for in good faith, because I believed the work mattered. I had made commitments to counterparts, to partners, to members of my own team, based on an effort that somebody above me already knew would not happen. When the reason finally came out, the explanation was reasonable. The feeling wasn't. You cannot reset an entire team's belief that their work is real with a single apology, no matter how well-intentioned.

Because once you realize you've been sent to chase something that was never meant to go anywhere, the next time it happens, you don't push harder. You hesitate. Or worse, you stop believing the work is real.

The meetings existed. But they were not real.

This wasn't a case of misalignment. It wasn't a failure of structure. The process itself was functioning exactly as designed, just not for the purpose everyone in the room believed.

Every organization that has ever held a planning cycle nobody believed in, run a strategy off-site after the strategy had already been decided, or put a team through a reorganization that was announced as consultation, has run some version of this. The people in the room usually know. They participate anyway, because participating is what the job appears to require. And while the meeting costs are not visible that afternoon, they show up later, in how seriously anyone takes the next meeting, and the one after that.

The Meeting Designed to Delay

I encountered another version of this dynamic on a different effort, though the cause was entirely different.

It was a multi-organization initiative, and this was the first time both teams sat down with the person who would lead the joint organization. By then, both sides had already made significant progress. The expectation for the meeting was straightforward: align on where each team stood, surface gaps, and begin defining how the work would come together going forward.

That part happened. Each team walked through their work. The differences became immediately visible — not in a confrontational way, but clearly enough that they would need to be worked through.

That was expected. What wasn't expected was what came next.

Instead of focusing on those points of misalignment, the conversation began drifting. Questions came in but not the ones you would expect at that level. They weren't about integration, or how to reconcile the differences that had just been surfaced, or how decisions would be made when the organizations disagreed — the things that would have actually determined whether the project could move forward. Instead the conversation kept landing on details that, whatever their technical merit, had no bearing on the fundamental questions the meeting was supposed to resolve.

Individually, none of these questions were wrong. But in that moment, they were irrelevant.

At one point, a member of their team stood up, walked to the whiteboard, and began breaking down a cost estimate in detail, line by line. It wasn't the first time he had done it. Each time he stood up, you could feel the room shift. People glanced at each other, leaned back in their chairs, looked down at their phones. More than once, someone caught another person's eye across the table — the kind of look that doesn't need words.

No one stopped it. The person leading the meeting didn't redirect the conversation. He followed it, asking more questions, going deeper into areas that had no impact on the decisions that actually needed to be made.

Hours passed. Nothing moved. No decisions were made. No alignment was reached. The core issues identified at the beginning of the meeting remained untouched.

The reaction came as people walked out of the room. "What was that?" "We didn't get anything out of that." "That was a complete waste of time."

The meetings weren't failing — they were succeeding at what they were actually for. Behind the scenes, certain individuals were waiting for the existing director to be replaced so that someone aligned with their own organization could take over. Until that happened, there was little incentive to allow the work to move forward. The meetings weren't designed to resolve questions. They were designed to consume time until the outcome that certain people were waiting for could arrive.

Once you see the theater, you stop believing the outcome will be anything but what someone else already decided.

What This Does Over Time

These situations go far beyond the ordinary frustration of an inefficient meeting. A legitimate meeting moves things forward. Not every meeting needs to produce a major decision, but it should clarify a question, surface a constraint, or advance the team's understanding. Even informational meetings serve a purpose when they build the trust and familiarity that accelerates later collaboration.

The situations described above did none of that. They created the opposite effect.

When meetings stop producing real outcomes, the change in people is gradual but predictable. After several cycles where discussions fail to lead to decisions, expectations adjust. Preparation becomes mechanical. The focus shifts from solving the problem to surviving the meeting.

Fewer ideas are brought forward. Less effort is invested in refining recommendations. Not because the team lacks capability but because experience has taught them that the outcome was never theirs to influence.

Eventually, the meeting becomes something to get through rather than something to contribute to. And once that happens, the organization loses access to the full thinking of the people involved.

People start to feel that their time is being used to maintain appearances rather than to make progress. They stop believing that the meeting is where the real conversation happens.

And belief, it turns out, is not a soft concept. It is the difference between a team that brings its full capability to a problem and a team that has learned to wait for permission that never comes.

The Leader's Responsibility

This does not mean leaders should always disclose every piece of information affecting an effort. There are situations — acquisitions, legal matters, confidential negotiations — where certain realities cannot be openly discussed. That is a legitimate constraint.

But when meetings cease to serve their intended purpose, leaders should recognize the cost that dynamic creates for the people involved. Organizations depend on the energy and commitment of the people working within them. When those individuals begin to feel that the process around them is artificial, the motivation that drives strong performance begins to fade.

At the foundation of any functioning organization is something deceptively simple: meetings must be places where real conversations happen and real decisions get made.

When that connection disappears, the organization does not stop immediately. But it begins losing something much harder to restore than time or money.

It loses confidence that the process will produce a real outcome.

And once that confidence is gone, people stop showing up to be heard. Rebuilding it requires leaders who are willing to make the process real again by making real decisions, in real rooms, with real consequences.

Watch for meetings that circle without converging. Analysis is presented, questions are answered, objections addressed. Everyone leaves with the sense that nothing actually happened. The visible tell: people looking at phones, because whatever is on those screens has become more interesting than what is happening in the room.

Distinguish meetings that struggle from meetings designed not to reach alignment. Some meetings fail because the problem is hard. Others succeed at their actual purpose: consuming time until the outcome certain people are waiting for arrives. When the discussion drifts away from the questions that matter, pay attention to why.

Notice what happens to a team's energy over repeated cycles. When meetings consistently fail to produce real outcomes, preparation becomes mechanical. People stop investing in refining recommendations because experience has taught them the outcome was never theirs to influence.

Recognize the cost of misdirected effort, even when it's justified. When leadership knows an effort won't proceed but can't disclose the reason, the team still pays. A single explanation after the fact, however reasonable, does not reset a team's belief that their work matters.

Chapter 10

Culture Is a Competitive Advantage, Until It Isn't

I worked, early in my career, for someone who said the same thing so consistently it became part of how the team operated.

"Bring the bad news early. Always."

He didn't say it once in an all-hands meeting and move on. He said it in one-on-ones, in project reviews, in casual conversations. He said it often enough that it stopped feeling like a directive and started feeling like a shared value, something the team understood not because they had been told to, but because they had seen what happened when they did.

What happened was this: problems got solved before they became catastrophic and mistakes got corrected before they compounded.

Someone on the team might surface a concern — a risk identified, a number that wasn't adding up, a decision that looked questionable in light of new information. Or they might come forward with something that had already gone wrong.

One time, the wrong set of valves had been installed and was starting to cause issues with the product. The team gathered quickly, assessed the situation, and found a solution. The person responsible knew what had happened and knew the team was there to help fix it, not to punish him for it. No one berated him. He learned his lesson, and everyone moved forward.

What made that possible was not just the leader's words. It was what the team had seen happen, repeatedly, when someone brought a problem forward. The response was always the same: gather, assess, solve, move on. Nobody had to wonder whether transparency was safe. They had seen it be safe, enough times, that it had become instinct.

Everyone on the team understood that what happened to one of them could happen to any of them. That shared understanding created something beyond individual courage. It created collective ownership. Nobody hesitated to jump in and help, because helping was simply how the team operated.

Over time, a culture like that becomes self-reinforcing. The shared experience of operating with high accountability and mutual trust creates a standard that new members either adapt to or don't.

That standard was tested when someone joined the team who was, by any technical measure, a highly competent engineer. His capability was not in question. But he struggled to operate within a culture that required the kind of transparency and accountability described above, not because he was unwilling to perform, but because the way the team functioned was genuinely foreign to how he had learned to work.

The team felt it. The boss noticed it. He asked around, and eventually tasked me with monitoring the situation and making a recommendation. I was careful in that conversation, perhaps overly so. The boss noticed that hesitation too.

When I finally laid down the hard facts, I recommended termination. The boss agreed. The person was let go with a decent severance, a short tenure, handled with integrity.

What that experience illustrated was something important about strong cultures: they don't maintain themselves automatically. They require leaders who are willing to notice when something is off, investigate it honestly, and make the hard call when the evidence warrants it while still treating people with decency throughout.

That is what a healthy culture around truth actually looks like in practice. Not a policy. Not a value statement on a wall. A repeated behavior from a leader that gradually became a shared instinct across the team, and a willingness to protect that culture when it was tested.

How Culture Breaks Down

Culture breaks down in the exact opposite direction.

Not dramatically. Not through a policy change or a visible decision. Through the gradual accumulation of small signals that teach people, just as reliably, that bringing the bad news early is no longer safe.

A concern gets raised and the response is defensive. A risk gets surfaced and the messenger gets managed rather than the message. An uncomfortable truth gets presented and the meeting moves on as if it hadn't been said.

Nobody announces that the culture has changed. But the team notices. And they adjust.

At first the changes are subtle. Conversations become more cautious. Certain topics begin to disappear from meetings. People hesitate before raising concerns that might complicate the discussion.

The problem is rarely that people suddenly stop seeing issues. It is that they stop talking about them.

I saw this play out at a young industrial company with real promise, genuine talent, and significant investor backing. The newly appointed project director had a feeling something wasn't quite right and brought me in as an outside advisor for a second set of eyes.

The first thing I noticed was how nice everyone was. Not professionally courteous — genuinely, almost unusually nice. The kind of team where meetings ran smoothly, voices stayed calm, and nobody ever seemed to leave a room in disagreement.

That was the first warning sign.

I started probing. I asked questions about subjects with clear, uncomfortable answers and watched how people responded. What I found was that these were genuinely good people who had, somewhere along the way, decided that getting along mattered more than getting it right. Agreement had become the goal. Harmony had replaced honesty. Nobody was lying, exactly, but nothing was said directly either. The truth was always in there somewhere, wrapped in enough softening and indirection that you had to interpret your way to it. I learned quickly that I could never take anything at face value. Every conversation required reading between the lines to figure out what was actually being said.

What I was looking at was something I have come to think of as *toxic positivity*. The unspoken rule was that everyone had to feel good, all the time, and that maintaining that feeling mattered more than the facts on the ground. It was never stated. It didn't need to be. It had been enforced, gradually and consistently, through the way the room responded whenever someone said something uncomfortable — a slight tension, a redirect, a change of subject. People had learned to read those signals. Most had stopped testing them. If you named something that was wrong, you weren't surfacing a problem, you were being a problem. The discomfort your words created in the room was treated as the thing that needed to be fixed, not the situation that had produced them.

That is the part that makes it toxic. Not the optimism itself. Optimism is fine. The problem is the inversion — a system that protects feelings at the expense of truth, and treats the people willing to name hard things as the ones disrupting the culture.

Nobody is suggesting that leaders should make people feel bad on purpose. Concerns can and should be raised respectfully. But an organization that worries more about protecting comfort than moving the work forward will never actually move the work forward. It will only get better at describing the lack of progress in encouraging language.

And that is what eventually shows up in the reports. A risk gets described as "manageable" rather than significant. A schedule concern becomes a "challenge" rather than a potential delay. Over time, the language itself begins masking reality. Leaders reviewing the situation see a series of manageable challenges rather than a collection of growing risks. The effort continues moving forward. But the clarity that should guide decision-making gradually disappears.

Nobody in the room is lying. Everyone in the room is adjusting.

The company later released a new set of values emphasizing being nice and being team players. In practice, it was a formalization of the problem. People would agree in meetings and then disregard the agreement the moment they walked out the door.

At the center of it was a vice president (VP) who, by all appearances, was an engaging and agreeable leader. He would listen carefully, ask good questions, look you in the eye, and tell you he was fully on board. And then he would walk out the door and do something entirely different.

It was not hostility. It was not even dishonesty in any way most people would recognize in the moment. It was a pattern — a consistent gap between what was said and what was done, wrapped in enough warmth and professionalism that it took time to see it for what it was. By the time you did, you had already committed to a direction he had quietly abandoned.

The project director saw it clearly. He had tried, more than once, to name what was actually happening on the project rather than what the VP preferred to hear. The relationship between them had been deteriorating for some time. At one point, in a private conversation, the VP had promised the director that if it ever came to the worst, he would be allowed to resign with dignity.

That promise was still in the air when the director organized an off-site team-building day for his project group. The morning after, he had invited me and the engineering manager over for a working session. It was a Friday morning. It was informal, but real work. We were set up in his garage around a high table, going through the next steps when he mentioned he had a call scheduled with his boss. Nothing unusual. He expected it to take about half an hour.

He stepped away to take it in his office.

He was back in less than ten minutes.

The moment he walked in, something felt off. Not dramatic, just wrong. His expression was controlled, but unsettled. The kind of look where you know something has shifted before anything is said.

He walked up to us and said it plainly.

"I just got fired."

No buildup. No explanation.

Just that.

He paused for a moment, then added, almost as a courtesy, "You guys are okay. Feel free to stay and finish your work. But I can't be part of it anymore."

Before either of us could respond, he turned and walked away, already dialing his phone.

A few minutes later, a meeting notification came through.

Urgent.

We joined.

The VP went straight to the point. The director had been let go. The reason given was that he was "not being a team player". One day after he had brought the entire team together.

There was a brief pause for questions.

You could hear it in people's voices, the shift. Not loud. Not chaotic. But present. Concern, confusion, calculation. Questions about the project, about the team, and more than anything, about what this meant for them.

Most of it was deferred.

There would be another meeting. More information would be shared then. A new director had already been selected and would be starting the following Monday.

That was the part that landed.

Not just that he was gone. But that the decision had already been made, the replacement already in place, and everything else was just catching up to it. The promise of a dignified exit, made in private months earlier, had somehow stopped applying somewhere along the way, and nobody had told him.

The call ended quickly.

No one said anything after.

Not on our end.

We were still in his house.

The work in front of us didn't matter anymore. The conversation we had been having just minutes earlier felt disconnected from what had just happened. We packed up shortly after and left.

There wasn't much to say on the way out. What we had been doing that morning — the real work, around a real table, with a director who was invested in it — had been made retroactively pointless by a phone call that took less than ten minutes. I kept thinking about the team-building day the day before. About how much of himself he had put into it, in front of people who had no idea what was about to happen. None of that was going to be remembered the way it was meant to be remembered. The organization had already rewritten the story of the previous twenty-four hours before any of us had a chance to process it.

People called me in the weeks that followed. They were trying to understand what had just happened and what it meant for them. Should they stay or leave? Was the company going to survive this? Was the project ever going to happen?

They were in freefall. The VP had just shown everyone what happens when you tell the truth, and they were trying to decide whether they could still work in that environment. None of them could point to anything that made staying feel safe. The trust wasn't damaged. It was gone.

A new director came in. Things did not improve. The same culture that had made honest conversation impossible did not change because the person at the top of the project changed. It couldn't. Everyone on that team had already seen what happens when you tell the truth — the director had been the one person willing to name what was actually happening, and he had been removed for it.

Months later, the project team was laid off. Eventually, the CEO was replaced. The company had been doing what the culture had taught it to do — maintaining appearances, protecting comfort, describing the lack of progress in encouraging language — and by the time someone forced the conversation, there was little left to save.

Leadership misalignment rarely stays contained between two individuals. It radiates outward. When commitments are reversed, when messaging contradicts lived experience, and when people begin questioning whether leadership means what it says, morale begins to fracture.

And fractured morale is extraordinarily difficult to repair. You can replace a leader. You can replace a plan. But once people begin doubting the credibility of leadership itself, performance becomes secondary. Because no team performs at its best inside ambiguity and distrust.

Culture Is the Foundation

Governance structures can define authority. Processes can define workflows. Meetings can organize discussion. But none of those mechanisms guarantee that people will speak honestly about what they see.

That willingness depends on culture — on whether individuals believe that raising difficult issues will be treated as a contribution to solving the problem or as a disruption to the narrative leadership prefers.

When organizations lose that distinction, they become fragile in a specific way. The technical work may still be excellent. The reporting systems may function exactly as designed. Yet the organization gradually loses access to the most important input it needs to make good decisions: reality.

Strong cultures do not eliminate problems. They make problems visible early. Early discomfort is far less expensive than late surprises.

This is why the most effective leaders consistently reinforce a principle that is simple to state and difficult to sustain: truth is more valuable than comfort.

Culture is a competitive advantage. But only when it is actively built, consistently protected, and honestly maintained. When it breaks down through neglect, through fear, or through the slow accumulation of signals that make honesty feel dangerous, it takes down everything built on top of it.

The next time someone brings you news you don't want to hear, you have a choice. What you do with it in that moment, in front of whoever is watching, will teach your organization more about its culture than anything you have ever said or written. That moment, is the culture.

Watch for agreement that has replaced honesty. Meetings that run smoothly with no disagreement. Truth wrapped in enough softening that you have to interpret your way to it. Nobody in the room is lying. Everyone in the room is adjusting.

Pay attention to what happens when someone tells the truth. If the system punishes someone for surfacing reality, the lesson is received by everyone who witnessed it, not just the person removed. What you do with uncomfortable information in front of whoever is watching will teach your organization more about its culture than anything you've ever said or written.

Recognize that culture is the repeated behavior, not the stated value. When someone surfaces a mistake and the team fixes it rather than assigns blame, everyone watching learns that honesty is safe. That learning is the culture.

Part IV —
Leadership in Practice

The failure sequence is not inevitable. It is preventable by leaders who understand what they actually control and are willing to act on it.

Chapter 11

The Leader's Real Job

It is not about you. Even if it is.

It would be convenient to say that great leaders are simply selfless. That they subordinate their own interests to the people they lead, the organizations they serve, and the outcomes they are responsible for. That version is clean, and it sounds right, and it is also incomplete.

Because leaders who get to positions of real consequence — who build organizations, shape industries, carry significant responsibility — almost always wanted to get there. They pursued it. They sacrificed for it. They navigated the obstacles and the politics and the long stretches of uncertainty that stand between ambition and achievement.

There is nothing wrong with that. Wanting to lead is not a character flaw. It is often the precondition for doing it well.

But here is what the most effective leaders eventually understand, some early, some only after expensive mistakes:

The ambition is best served by directing the energy outward.

Not because selflessness is morally superior. But because of how organizations, teams, and markets actually work. The leader who wants the position must persuade people that their work will be better, their outcomes stronger, their efforts more meaningful for having followed. The company that wants to generate wealth must first create something people want badly enough to pay for. The leader who wants to be trusted must first demonstrate that they can be trusted with something that matters to someone else.

You get what you are after — the position, the impact, the legacy — by making other people successful first.

That is not a sacrifice of ambition. It is the mechanism of it.

The measure of a leader's power is not the authority they hold but the number of people willing to stand behind them. Authority is assigned. Power — real power, the kind that actually moves organizations — is given. Continuously, by the people who choose to follow. And the moment they stop choosing, it disappears regardless of what the title says.

The patterns described throughout this book are not leadership failures in the abstract. They are what happens when the conditions are wrong. And the conditions are never set by accident.

What Leaders Actually Control

Leadership is often misunderstood, and at nearly every level, leaders tend to believe they control far more than they actually do.

A senior sponsor has very little direct control over the details of any complex effort. They are not deciding how systems are designed or how day-to-day execution unfolds. Yet they set direction, define objectives, and above all, choose the people who will lead the effort. That alone influences almost everything that follows.

Further down the organization, directors and managers operate closer to execution. They have more visibility, more involvement in decisions, and more influence over how work progresses. And still, the same misconception appears: the belief that they can control everything.

They cannot.

One of the most common mistakes in leadership is believing you can control people. You can apply pressure, enforce decisions, and use authority, but none of that creates commitment. At best, it produces compliance. And compliance is fragile. It holds only as long as the pressure remains.

What leaders actually control is the conditions under which people operate. They set direction, establish expectations, shape behavior, and define what is acceptable and what is not. They influence how decisions are made and create the environment in which those decisions take place.

That is the real scope of leadership.

And most of the time, the discipline required is not technical. One of the hardest lessons to accept, especially for leaders with deep technical backgrounds, is that most organizational problems are not technical problems at all. They are people problems. Not because people lack capability, but because they bring everything with them into the work: their experiences, pressures, incentives, frustrations, and ambitions. None of that stays outside the door.

Leaders who ignore that reality tend to struggle. They end up solving the wrong problem.

Being Right Is Not Enough

I watched this play out with a very capable leader.

He was experienced, structured, and deeply knowledgeable. He understood governance, process, and how the effort should operate. He was right — intellectually and procedurally right — which is precisely what made the situation so difficult to watch.

He was trying to enforce the correct way of doing things in an organization that was operating very differently. He approached it directly. He pushed for alignment with process, pointed to the structure, and challenged deviations.

From a technical standpoint, everything he was doing made sense.

But the environment he was operating in was not purely technical. It was political. And that changes the game entirely.

He was trying to win an intellectual argument inside an emotional and political system. That is a losing position no matter how correct the argument is.

Over time, resistance grew. Friction increased. Relationships deteriorated. Eventually he lost the support he needed to continue and was let go. Not because he was wrong. But because he could not influence the system he was operating within.

That is one of the more uncomfortable realities of leadership: being right is not enough. Leaders must be able to navigate the environment in which they actually operate. That does not mean compromising integrity or abandoning standards. But it does mean understanding how decisions are actually made, not just how they should be made. Sometimes the most effective path is not direct. It requires building alignment, not forcing it, and allowing others to arrive at conclusions rather than proving them wrong.

On one project I was responsible for the owner's engineering team. We were moving fast. Decisions had to be made. And my team couldn't move without them.

The bottleneck was a single person.

On paper, he was a director of operations.

In practice, he carried far more weight than that.

He had been instrumental in getting the deal done that led to the project. The company trusted him. He had relationships and influence inside and beyond the organization. And at some point, it seemed he had expected to be the one leading the project.

That didn't happen.

The company brought in an experienced project director instead, someone whose role was to deliver what the business needed, not what any one individual wanted.

That created tension.

Not open conflict. Something more controlled.

He wasn't trying to stop the project. He needed it to succeed as much as anyone. But he was trying to shape it — timing decisions, controlling when things moved, making sure they aligned with how he wanted the outcome to unfold.

On a longer timeline, it might have worked.

But in the moment, it meant that nothing moved when it needed to.

From where I sat, it felt like resistance.

My team needed decisions. We needed clarity. And we weren't getting it.

So I did what had worked for me before.

I went direct.

And when that didn't work, I started building alignment outside of him. Reaching out to people who had decision authority. Connecting pieces that weren't being connected. And eventually, I forced the issue into a room that couldn't be avoided.

The president of the company was there.

He was there too.

That mattered.

Because this was someone who was used to controlling when conversations happened. Skipping meetings when it suited him. Letting things stretch when it created leverage.

This time, he didn't have that option.

The meeting started.

I laid everything out, clearly, directly, without much room for interpretation. What we needed. What was missing. What the impact was.

From an execution standpoint, it was straightforward.

And it worked.

The decision was made. And made at a level he couldn't override. The path forward was cleared. My team could move.

In that moment, I had done exactly what I set out to do.

Toward the end of the meeting, he spoke.

Calm. Measured. Polished.

He said that moving forward, it would be best if we worked things out directly before escalating matters like this. That we should align beforehand rather than bringing issues up at that level.

To anyone listening casually, it sounded reasonable.

Collaborative, even.

But that wasn't what it was.

What he was really saying was: don't go around me again.

And I knew it.

At the time, I didn't think much of it.

From my perspective, the project had what it needed. The work could continue. The problem was solved.

What I didn't fully appreciate was that I hadn't just solved a problem.

I had disrupted how he intended to shape the outcome.

And I had done it publicly.

That mattered more than I understood at the time.

I was operating purely on what was best for the company. I didn't have a personal stake beyond delivering the work correctly and maintaining my own standards. I was on a contract. Once the job was done, I was out.

He wasn't.

He was playing a longer game.

And I had stepped into it without realizing the full implications.

He didn't respond in that moment.

He didn't need to.

He had more history in the organization. More relationships. More reach. I had earned visibility, but I didn't have the same foundation.

When the opportunity came, he used it.

It didn't look like retaliation.

It never does.

It looked like a shift in direction. A change in priorities. A realignment of responsibilities.

And I was no longer part of it.

At the time, it was frustrating.

From my perspective, I had done exactly what the project required. I had removed a constraint. I had delivered the outcome.

And I had.

But I had done it in a way that ignored the system I was operating in.

I had forced the result instead of shaping it.

And in doing so, I made myself part of the problem.

That was the lesson.

You can be right.

You can be effective.

You can even get the outcome.

And still lose.

The deeper lesson, the one that took me longer to see, was not about tactics. It was about diagnosis. I had solved the wrong problem. I thought I was solving a stalled decision. I was actually inside a question about who the project belonged to, and I had answered it publicly, in a room with the president, on behalf of someone who had not asked me to.

Every tactical choice I made that day was correct for the problem I thought I was solving. And wrong for the problem I was actually in.

What It Looks Like When the Conditions Are Right

I want to describe a specific meeting, not because the technical details matter, but because of what it showed about what leadership actually produces when it works.

We had developed a proposal and brought it to a broad group for review. The room contained people from multiple functions, each with their own priorities and constraints. The director responsible for the effort was present but not leading the discussion.

What he did instead was watch. And intervene, but only in specific ways.

When the discussion built productive momentum, he let it run. He did not step in to validate or redirect. He trusted the room to work through the problem.

When someone raised a concern, he received it with curiosity rather than defense. He asked questions. He allowed the issue to be examined fully before the group moved on.

When the tone shifted — when the discussion began drifting toward something personal rather than something productive — he addressed it immediately. Not formally. Directly. A quick reset, a reminder to stay focused on the problem. That was enough.

What he never did was use his position to shut anything down. He never made it feel like the direction had already been decided. He never undermined anyone in the room, even when he disagreed.

The result was a discussion that tested the proposal thoroughly, and improved it significantly. The final outcome was better than what we had brought in. The director hadn't driven it there. He had created the conditions for the room to get there on its own.

After that meeting, we stayed in the conversation. We kept reaching out as questions arose. We tested assumptions while they were still flexible. By the time we presented again, very little felt new. Most people had already been part of shaping the direction.

That is a very different conversation than the one where a finished recommendation meets a room full of people hearing it for the first time.

The Discipline of Consistency

What makes those environments work is not a single trait. It is a pattern of behavior that shows up consistently over time.

Strong leaders expect performance. Mediocrity does not last long when the standard is clear. But what distinguishes the most effective leaders is how they respond when things go wrong.

Mistakes happen. Decisions are made with incomplete information. Assumptions prove wrong. The strongest leaders do not stay in the reaction. They come back, re-engage, and focus the conversation on understanding what happened and what needs to change.

They recognize performance, but only when it is earned. They remain attentive to what their people need, not just in terms of tasks but in terms of conditions. They hold legal, ethical, and moral lines without exception. And they know what to engage with and what to let pass, staying focused on what actually drives the outcome while acting quickly when something begins affecting the system.

That selectivity keeps the organization centered on what actually matters.

The Contrast

One organization I worked with was running multiple projects at the same time. Two of those projects were operating almost side by side — same building, similar conditions, similar level of complexity. Each had its own director, its own structure, and its own team underneath.

From the outside, you would have expected similar outcomes. Both teams were made up of competent people. Both directors were experienced, senior individuals who had led similar efforts before. Neither team had been handed an ideal situation. They each had their own challenges to work through, different in nature but comparable in weight.

And yet, as time went on, the difference in performance became impossible to ignore.

One team consistently moved forward. There was a rhythm to how they worked. Decisions were made. Problems were addressed quickly. Work didn't stall waiting for perfect alignment. There was structure, but it didn't get in the way. Conversations happened informally when needed. People would walk into each other's offices, resolve issues quickly, and then bring things back into the formal channels afterward. The system supported the work, but it didn't slow it down.

The other team struggled. Progress was slower, and not because the work itself was more difficult. It was slower because everything required coordination through formal channels. Decisions didn't happen in the room — they had to be escalated, reviewed, confirmed. Bottlenecks appeared everywhere. Work would pause, waiting on approvals, waiting on alignment, waiting on clarity that never seemed to come fast enough.

What made it more striking was that the team that spent more time physically together, the one that was in the building more frequently, was the one underperforming.

When both teams happened to be in the building at the same time, people talked. There was no hostility between them. If anything, there was curiosity. And eventually, the questions started coming.

"What are you guys doing differently?" "How are you able to move that fast?" "How are you getting decisions made without all the back and forth?"

Those weren't casual questions. They were coming from people who were feeling the friction inside their own system and could see, just across the hall, that something else was working better.

We shared what we were doing. There was nothing secret about it. After all, both teams worked for the same company. It wasn't a different process or a different tool. It was simply how the team operated — how decisions were made, how communication flowed, how much autonomy people had to move the work forward without waiting for permission at every step.

And to their credit, parts of that other team did improve. At the working level, you could see individuals and smaller groups starting to adopt some of those behaviors. Things got a bit faster. Some bottlenecks eased.

But the overall system didn't change. Because at the top, the leadership still held tightly to control. Decisions still had to pass through the same narrow points. Alignment was still something that had to be formally validated before anything moved forward.

And that became the limiting factor.

You can grow, or you can control, but you cannot fully do both. At some point, if everything has to pass through you, you become the bottleneck.

That's exactly what happened.

By the time one team delivered what they were supposed to deliver, the gap between the two had become difficult to ignore. The difference wasn't talent. It wasn't resources. It wasn't even the complexity of the work. It was how the system allowed, or prevented, the work from moving.

One was organized to move. The other was organized to control, and over time, that difference compounded.

The Conditions Are Everything

When all of this comes together, the effect is not dramatic. There is no single turning point where everything changes. Instead, the organization begins to operate differently. People engage more freely. Information moves more easily. Problems surface earlier. Decisions become clearer not because the work itself is easier, but because the environment supports the work.

People do not wait to be told what to do. They engage. They think ahead. They raise issues before they become problems. And they do it without hesitation, because they trust the system around them.

That trust is not accidental. It is built through repetition, through consistency, through the accumulated evidence that the leader means what they say and does what they commit to.

There are no perfect organizations. There never will be. But there are organizations where the conditions are strong enough that people bring everything they have to the work, and there are organizations where those conditions are not present.

That difference is not accidental.

It is created and sustained, decision by decision, behavior by behavior, through the discipline of leadership.

Not control. Not authority. Not the appearance of alignment.

The creation of conditions where capable people can do their best work and where reality is allowed to move freely through the system.

That is the leader's real job.

And it starts with understanding one thing clearly:

It is not about you.

Even if it is.

Recognize the difference between compliance and commitment. Compliance is produced by pressure and holds only as long as the pressure remains. Commitment is produced by conditions. Leaders control the conditions, not the outcomes. That is the actual scope of leadership.

Understand that being right is not enough. A leader can be correct on substance and still lose the position because they couldn't influence the system they were operating within. Diagnose the actual problem before acting. A stalled decision and a question about ownership require different responses.

Watch how you intervene. When the discussion builds momentum, let it run. When someone raises a concern, receive it with curiosity. When the tone shifts toward something personal, redirect immediately. Never use your position to shut something down or make it feel like the direction was already decided.

Organize to move, not to control. When everything has to pass through one person, that person becomes the bottleneck. You can grow or you can control, but you cannot fully do both.

Chapter 12

The Next Time You See It

By the time you reach this point, none of what you've read should feel unfamiliar.

If anything, it should feel recognizable.

You've seen these patterns before. You've been in those meetings. You've felt that hesitation, that misalignment, that moment where something wasn't quite right but no one said it out loud.

In most of the situations described in this book, someone in the room knew what was happening.

They just didn't say it. Or they didn't act on it.

And now, you likely recognize it more clearly.

Not motivated. Not inspired. Responsible.

There's a moment that happens when something clicks, when what used to feel vague suddenly becomes obvious. It's not always comfortable. It usually does the opposite. It creates a kind of internal pressure that doesn't go away until something changes.

That's the feeling. Not frustration for its own sake. But a steady understanding that something needs to be done, and that you may be one of the few people in the room who actually sees it.

Once you see these patterns clearly, you don't get to ignore them anymore. You don't get to sit in the room and pretend everything is fine when it isn't. You don't get to participate in the same cycles without recognizing your role in them.

Understanding this is not the hard part. Applying it is.

Because nothing about this is as straightforward as it seems.

If you are building an organization from scratch, you have an advantage. You can shape the environment. You can hire deliberately. You can set expectations early and reinforce them consistently.

But most people don't operate in that world. Most people work inside organizations that already exist — with history, with politics, with incentives that have been shaped over time in ways that reward caution more than clarity, compliance more than truth, and survival more than performance.

Those systems don't change because you read a book. They don't change because you walk into the office on Monday morning with a new perspective.

If you try to apply everything here all at once, directly and without context, you will likely fail. Or worse, you will succeed in the moment and pay for it later — you've already seen what that looks like.

So don't count on that. Don't count on showing up tomorrow and fixing everything you now see. This is not a one-time shift. It is a pattern of behavior, repeated consistently, over time.

The most practical way to start is smaller than most people expect.

If you are responsible for a team, start there. Create the environment within your own scope. Ask the questions others avoid. Verify alignment instead of assuming it. Make it safe for people to speak, but not optional for them to engage. Be political when you have to be. Avoid the common pitfalls. Work this in the background until you don't have to work it in the background anymore.

You've already seen what happens when one team operates this way inside a larger organization. The contrast becomes visible. The questions start coming. And those questions, asked by people who can feel the friction in their own system, are worth more than any mandate from the top.

At first, it won't feel different. Then it will. And when it does, the results will follow — not because you forced them, but because the system around you begins to function differently.

That is how this spreads. Not through mandates. Through results.

Here is what I can tell you for certain.

Sometime this week, you are going to sit in a meeting and feel one of the patterns from this book. You will recognize it. You will know which chapter it came from. And you will have a choice you didn't have a month ago.

It might be a dashboard whose green indicators don't quite match what you're hearing in the hallway. It might be a question that everyone in the room is carefully not asking. It might be a decision that's being made for reasons no one is willing to put on the table. It might be a meeting that has been going for forty minutes and hasn't produced a single thing that will outlast the room.

You will see it. You won't be able to unsee it.

And then you will have a few seconds to decide whether to say something.

Most people, most of the time, won't. That is the honest part. The pull of self-preservation is real, and it is not a moral failure to feel it. I have felt it. I have given in to it. I have left rooms thinking I should have said something and didn't.

But every once in a while, someone does say it. Not perfectly. Not all at once. Just enough to shift the direction of the room by a few degrees. And those few degrees, accumulated across a career, are most of what separates the leaders whose organizations succeed from the ones whose organizations don't.

The patterns don't go away.

I have watched them repeat across organizations, industries, and decades. Hundreds of millions of dollars in value destroyed, by behaviors that were visible early and never properly addressed.

That part doesn't change. Human nature doesn't change. Left on their own, people will protect themselves.

They will avoid risk. They will defer decisions that carry consequences. They will choose comfort over clarity more often than they should.

That's not a flaw. It's predictable.

But it's also not the whole story. Because every once in a while, someone sees it, and instead of going along with it, they do something about it. Not perfectly. Not all at once. But enough to shift the direction.

That's why I keep doing this work. Not because the problems are new, but because they are visible. Because they are preventable. And because the difference between an organization that succeeds and one that struggles often comes down to whether someone in the room is willing to acknowledge what's actually happening, and act on it.

You already know more than you think. You've seen these patterns. You've felt them. You've likely been part of them.

The difference now is that you can recognize them for what they are.

And once you can do that, the question is no longer whether they exist.

It's what you're going to do this week, when you see one.

Because you will.

Start within the scope you control. The system you walk back into Monday morning rewards caution over clarity, compliance over truth. You won't change it by applying everything at once. Start smaller than you think you should.

Let results do the convincing. When one team operates differently inside a larger organization, the contrast becomes visible. Questions start coming from people who feel the friction in their own systems. Those questions carry more weight than any mandate from above.

Accept that most people won't. You will see the pattern, you won't be able to unsee it, and you will have a few seconds to decide whether to say something. Most people, most of the time, won't. The difference is made by the person who does. Not perfectly. Not all at once. Just enough to shift the direction of the room by a few degrees.

Acknowledgments

This book has been forming over many years, across projects, conversations, and moments that didn't make sense at the time but stayed with me. What appears here is the result of seeing those moments repeat often enough that they stopped feeling like isolated issues and started to look like patterns.

I am grateful to the people I have worked with over the years, the colleagues, counterparts, clients, and contractors who appear in these pages in some form, whether they realized it or not. Some of those stories are uncomfortable to tell. All of them are told with respect for the people involved and recognition that I was not always the one who saw it clearly first.

I am especially grateful to my wife Celeste, whose patience with this project outlasted its many false starts, and to my sons, Leonardo and Benjamin, who will one day encounter their own versions of everything described here. I hope this book gives them a head start.

I'd also like to thank Sak Forid Mohon for his work on the cover design, and Carlos Quiñones, Javier Torres, and Anthony Cruz, for their support in editing and refining this manuscript. Taking a book from a rough draft to a finished page is its own kind of complex effort, and I'm grateful to everyone who helped carry it forward.

Discussion Guide

A Guide for Teams and Leaders

These questions are designed for leadership teams reading this book together, to surface the conversations that don't always happen in formal settings.

Part I — Clarity

- Where in our current work would different people give different answers to "what are we trying to accomplish?" Have we actually checked?

- What decisions have we made recently that we are still treating as open questions? Are we advancing past them or resolving them?

- Who in our organization is responsible for holding the whole picture, the coherence of the whole? Can you name that person?

Part II — Truth

- What does it feel like to bring bad news to leadership here? What has happened in the past when someone did?

- Think of the last time a serious problem surfaced late. Where was it visible earlier — and why didn't it travel?

- When is the last time a disagreement in a meeting actually changed the outcome? What does that tell us?

Part III — The Threats

- Is the formal decision-making process the real one? If not, where do decisions actually get made?

- Are there meetings in your organization that exist to perform progress rather than make it? What would happen if they stopped?

- How would you describe your team's culture to someone who just joined? How would that person describe it after six months?

Part IV — Leadership

- What do you actually control as a leader — and what are you trying to control that you don't?

- Think of a moment where being right wasn't enough. What was the system you were actually operating in?

- What is one thing you now see more clearly that you didn't before reading this? What will you do differently this week?

About the Author

C ristian Gonzalez has spent more than twenty years inside complex industrial capital projects — in chemicals and polymers, oil and gas, and first-of-a-kind scale-up efforts — watching the same patterns of organizational failure repeat across companies, sectors, and decades. The work has ranged across five countries in North and South America, and from smaller capital initiatives to projects measured in the hundreds of millions.

He has led and consulted on major capital efforts from early conceptual design through execution, in joint ventures, corporate transformations, and early-stage companies. The patterns he writes about in this book are ones he has lived through, sometimes recognized in time, and sometimes only understood years later. He continues to advise senior leaders on the projects where the cost of getting it wrong is highest.

He lives in Houston, Texas, where he flies small aircraft and spends time with his family.

Work With the Author

The work described in this book is not confined to industrial projects. The patterns show up wherever leadership teams have lost clarity on what they are trying to accomplish, wherever truth has stopped reaching the people who need it, and wherever an effort is carrying more risk than anyone is willing to name out loud.

Cristian has spent more than twenty years inside those moments, across capital projects, post-acquisition integrations, scale-up transitions, and strategic transformations — in owner organizations, contractor environments, and early-stage ventures — across the United States, Mexico, Colombia, Canada, and the Caribbean. The settings vary. The underlying work is the same: restoring the conditions that allow capable people to make good decisions and move forward with confidence.

He has shaped or delivered over a billion dollars in capital investment, from early scope definition through execution, commissioning, and startup. He continues to advise senior leadership teams on the efforts where the cost of getting it wrong is highest.

For speaking engagements, advisory work, or bulk orders:

book@cristianygonzalez.com
www.cristianygonzalez.com

www.ingramcontent.com/pod-product-compliance
Lightning Source LLC
Chambersburg PA
CBHW020839150726
48196CB00002B/135